WADING INTO WETLANDS

OTHER TITLES IN *RANGER RICK'S NATURESCOPE*

AMAZING MAMMALS, PART I

AMAZING MAMMALS, PART II

ASTRONOMY ADVENTURES

BIRDS, BIRDS, BIRDS

DIGGING INTO DINOSAURS

DISCOVERING DESERTS

DIVING INTO OCEANS

ENDANGERED SPECIES: WILD & RARE

GEOLOGY: THE ACTIVE EARTH

INCREDIBLE INSECTS

LET'S HEAR IT FOR HERPS

POLLUTION: PROBLEMS & SOLUTIONS

RAIN FORESTS: TROPICAL TREASURES

TREES ARE TERRIFIC!

WILD ABOUT WEATHER

WILD & CRAFTY

Ranger Rick's NatureScope

WADING INTO WETLANDS

National Wildlife Federation

LEARNING TRIANGLE PRESS

*Connecting
kids, parents, and teachers
through learning*

An imprint of McGraw-Hill

New York San Francisco Washington, D.C. Auckland Bogotá Caracas
Lisbon London Madrid Mexico City Milan Montreal New Delhi
San Juan Singapore Sydney Tokyo Toronto

Library of Congress Cataloging-in-Publication Data applied for

McGraw-Hill

A Division of The McGraw·Hill Companies

NATIONAL WILDLIFE FEDERATION®

NatureScope® is published by Learning Triangle Press, an imprint of McGraw-Hill. Copyright 1997, 1989 by the National Wildlife Federation. All rights reserved. Permission is granted, without written request, to copy pages specified as "Copycat Pages," as well as those sections of the text specifically designated for student use. The reproduction of any other parts of this book is strictly prohibited without written permission from the publisher, McGraw-Hill. The publisher takes no responsibility for the use of any materials or methods described in this book, nor for the products thereof.

1 2 3 4 5 6 7 8 9 JDL/JDL 9 0 2 1 0 9 8 7

ISBN 0-07-046507-X

NatureScope® was originally conceived by National Wildlife Federation's School Programs Editorial Staff, under the direction of Judy Braus, Editor. Special thanks to all of the Editorial Staff, Scientific, Educational Consultants and Contributors who brought this series of eighteen publications to life.

NATIONAL WILDLIFE FEDERATION EDITORIAL STAFF
Creative Services Manager: Sharon Schiliro
Editor, Ranger Rick® magazine: Gerry Bishop
Director Classroom–related Programs: Margaret Tunstall
Contributors: Carol Boggis, Rhonda Lucas Donald, Sharon Levy, Susan Makurat–Bond

McGRAW-HILL EDP STAFF
Acquisitions Editor: Judith Terrill-Breuer
Editorial Supervisor: Patricia V. Amoroso
Production Supervisor: Claire Stanley
Designer: Jaclyn J. Boone
Cover Design: David Saylor

McGraw-Hill books are available at special quantity discounts to use as premiums and sales promotions, or for use in corporate training programs. For more information, please write to the Director of Special Sales, McGraw-Hill, 11 West 19th Street, New York, NY 10011. Or contact your local bookstore.

Printed and bound by the John D. Lucas Printing Company.
This book is printed on recycled and acid–free paper.

TM and ® designate trademarks of National Wildlife Federation and are used, under license, by The McGraw-Hill Companies, Inc.

RRNS

MEETING THE CHALLENGE

GOAL

Ranger Rick's Nature-Scope is a creative education series dedicated to inspiring in children an understanding and appreciation of the natural world while developing the skills they will need to make responsible decisions about the environment.

It has been almost a decade since the publication of the first *Wading Into Wetlands* in the **Ranger Rick's NatureScope** series. Since that time, we have had both encouraging and discouraging news about the environment. Our awareness has been heightened and much has been done, but there is still much to do.

One of the best ways to ensure sustained concern for our planet and the creatures who inhabit it is to educate our children. This new edition of *Wading Into Wetlands* brings to the classroom the original material which has survived the test of time, along with new essays by and about people working in the field today, people who are still learning about how our environment works and who are taking action to preserve it. Here also is the sense of wonder they feel as they work in the natural world. This new edition also includes an updated bibliography for further study and enrichment.

The effort to save wildlife and habitat will span many generations. Like all lifelong commitments, there is no better time to begin than when we are young.

National Wildlife Federation

TABLE OF CONTENTS

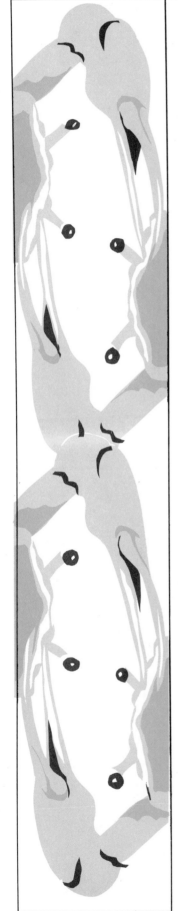

1. WHAT MAKES A WETLAND A WETLAND?..............................3

Describes the major characteristics of wetlands and why wetlands are valuable to wildlife and people.

ACTIVITIES.............................5
- Create a Scene
- Surveys and Slogans
- Explore a Wetland
- Wetland Models
- Put It on the Map!

COPYCAT PAGES...................14
- Create a Scene
- Explore a Wetland
- Put It on the Map!—Part 1
- Put It on the Map!—Part 2

2. SALTWATER WETLANDS........18

Looks at the characteristics of salt marshes and mangrove swamps and the plants and animals that live in them.

ACTIVITIES.............................21
- Make a Mud Snail
- Amazing Mangroves
- Salty Discoveries
- Build a Mangrove
- Changing with the Tide

COPYCAT PAGES...................30
- Make a Mud Snail
- Amazing Mangroves
- Changing with the Tide

3. FRESHWATER WETLANDS.....33

Focuses on the characteristics of freshwater swamps, marshes, and bogs.

ACTIVITIES.............................36
- Little Green Monsters
- Hidden in the Marsh
- Gator Hole Graphics

COPYCAT PAGES...................42
- Little Green Monsters
- Hidden in the Marsh
- Gator Hole Graphics—Part 1
- Gator Hole Graphics—Part 2

4. WETLANDS, WILDLIFE, AND PEOPLE..............................46

Takes a look at the ways people have used and abused wetlands and what we can do to help protect them.

ACTIVITIES.............................49
- From Marsh to Marina
- A Taste of Wetlands
- The Great Swamp Debate
- What's Your Wetland IQ?

COPYCAT PAGES...................56
- From Marsh to Marina
- The Great Swamp Debate
- What's Your Wetland IQ?

5. CRAFTY CORNER.................59
- Cattails for Kids
- This Pitcher's a Catcher!
- Wild Wetland Critters

6. APPENDIX.............................63
- Wetland Glossary
- Bibliography
—General Reference Books
—Field Guides
—Children's Books
—Films, Filmstrips, Records, Slide Sets, and Videos
—Booklets, Kits, Maps, and Posters
—Other Activity Sources
—Software
—Where to Get More Information
—Ranger Rick Wetland Index

1997 UPDATE

TABLE OF CONTENTS...........67

THE KISSIMMEE RIVER COMES HOME.......................69

PRAIRIE MAGIC.....................73

URBAN WETLANDS..............78

WETLANDS & WAL-MART......83

BIBLIOGRAPHY UPDATE.......87

A Close-Up Look At Wading Into Wetlands

ooking at the Table of Contents, you can see we've divided *Wading Into Wetlands* into four chapters (each of which deals with a broad wetland theme), a craft section, and an appendix. Each of the four chapters includes *background information* that explains concepts and vocabulary, *activities* that relate to the chapter theme, and *Copycat Pages* that reinforce many of the concepts introduced in the activities.

You can choose single activity ideas or teach each chapter as a unit. Either way, each activity stands by itself and includes teaching objectives, a list of materials needed, suggested age groups, subjects covered, and a step-by-step explanation of how to do the activity. (The objectives, materials, age groups, and subjects are highlighted in the left-hand margin for easy reference.)

AGE GROUPS

The suggested age groups are:

- Primary (grades K-2)
- Intermediate (grades 3-5)
- Advanced (grades 6-7)

Each chapter usually begins with primary activities and ends with intermediate or advanced activities. But don't feel bound by the grade levels we suggest. Resourceful teachers, naturalists, parents, and club leaders can adapt most of these activities to fit their particular age group and needs.

OUTDOOR ACTIVITIES

The best way to study a wetland is to visit one. Check with your state department of natural resources or your local park system to find out the locations of marshes, swamps, or bogs in your area. Also see "Explore a Wetland" on page 8 for tips about taking a wetland field trip with your group. It and other outdoor activities are coded in this issue with this symbol:

COPYCAT PAGES

The *Copycat Pages* supplement the activities and include ready-to-copy games, puzzles, coloring pages, and worksheets. *Answers to all Copycat Pages are in the texts of the activities.*

WHAT'S AT THE END

The fifth section, *Crafty Corner*, will give you some art and craft ideas that complement many of the activities in the first four chapters. And the last section, the *Appendix*, is loaded with reference suggestions that include books, films, and wetland posters. The *Appendix* also has a wetland glossary and suggestions of where to get more wetland information. (*Note:* The questions and answers, which normally appear in the Appendix, are in the activity called "What's Your Wetland IQ?" on pages 53-55.)

WHAT MAKES A WETLAND A WETLAND?

The water's up to your ankles and a pungent smell reaches your nose. You move along slowly, watching a great blue heron fish for its lunch. When you round a bend, you're startled by a flock of ducks as they take off from the water. A dragonfly zips past your head as you watch the ducks fly up over the trees.

You could be in a swamp. Or a salt marsh. Or any of a number of different types of wetlands. In this chapter we'll discuss just what we mean by the word *wetland*—and we'll look at what makes these soggy habitats so special.

WATERLOGGED WORLDS

It's hard to find a lot of absolute characteristics that apply to all wetlands. That's because there are so many different kinds of bogs, marshes, swamps, and other wetlands. (For descriptions of many of the different kinds of wetlands, see the background information on pages 18-20 and 33-35.) But all wetlands share some characteristics that set them apart from other kinds of habitats.

What They Are and What They Aren't: Of course, all wetlands are wet—but so are ponds, lakes, streams, rivers, and oceans. Does that mean, then, that these particular bodies of water are wetlands too?

In general, no. Most scientists who study wetlands restrict their definition of these habitats to areas that, at least periodically, have waterlogged soils or are covered with a relatively shallow layer of water. These areas support plants and animals that are adapted to living in a watery environment. (For more about the plants and animals that live in different kinds of wetlands, see Chapters 2 and 3.)

Soggy Surroundings: The reason that wetlands are wet varies. Since most wetlands are located in low-lying areas, rain and runoff help to keep them saturated. Also, some wetlands lie in places where the groundwater is at or very near the surface of the ground, which means that they're constantly being "fed" from below. Other wetlands stay wet because they're next to rivers or other bodies of water that regularly overflow their boundaries. And along the coast, the tides keep many other wetlands saturated.

Beavers and Other Builders: Some wetlands get started with a little "outside" help. Beavers, for example, are important wetland builders. The rivers and streams that they dam often flood large areas, turning meadows into marshes or parts of forests into swampland.

People sometimes create wetlands too—both intentionally and unintentionally. For example, a state game and fish agency might flood an area so that waterfowl will have more places to breed. On the other hand, a swamp or marsh might get its start accidentally when construction blocks the natural flow of water and causes a stream to back up and overflow.

WETLANDS AT WORK

Wetlands give the world a lot of "free services." Here's a look at some of the important functions they perform.

Flood Busters: An easy and cheap way of controlling floods is to leave wetlands in their natural state. That's because wetlands act like giant, shallow bowls. Water flowing into these "bowls" naturally loses velocity as it collects and spreads out.

(continued next page)

Wetland vegetation helps to slow down fast-moving water too. As a result, flood damage to developed areas near wetlands is often much less than damage to areas located near wetlands that have been drained and filled.

Silt Trappers: When flood waters are slowed by wetlands, the silt and other sediments they carry settle out among the roots and stems of wetland plants. This helps to protect streams, lakes, and other bodies of water downstream from a build-up of sediment that could otherwise clog aquatic animals' gills and bury their eggs. It also helps protect water supplies from pollutants and other impurities. That's because wetland plants can take up and use nutrients and chemicals that the silt may contain. If it weren't for wetlands, these impurities might eventually contaminate rivers, lakes, groundwater, and other water supplies—some of which are used as sources of drinking water. (For more about how wetlands can offset the effects of pollution, see "Don't Touch That Wetland" on page 48.)

Storm Breakers: Farms, forests, and buildings that are located behind wetlands along the seashore and large lakes often fare much better during storms than those that aren't. Wetlands serve as buffers between the winds and waves of storms and the areas beyond. But "taking the punishment" isn't all wetlands do during storms. They also bind soil and help to keep it from eroding. Mangrove swamps are particularly good at this. In fact, certain islands cleared of their mangrove swamps have become so severely eroded that they're no longer visible above the ocean's surface. (For more about mangrove swamps, see the background information on page 20.)

WETLANDS AND WILDLIFE

Acre for acre, there's more life in a healthy wetland than there is in almost any other kind of habitat. These productive places can support huge numbers of insects, fish, birds, and other animals. Below is a rundown of some of the ways wildlife uses wetlands.

Migration Vacations: If you visited a wetland in fall or spring, chances are you'd see many kinds of migrant birds. And depending on exactly where you were, you could see hundreds or even thousands of them: ducks and geese, herons and egrets, sandpipers and plovers; maybe even eagles and ospreys. These and other birds converge on wetlands en route to their winter or summer homes. Here they "refuel" on the rich food supply before getting on with their journeys. (Many birds nest and winter in wetlands too—but the bird population of most wetlands goes way up during migration.)

Natural Nurseries: There's another segment of wetland society for which wetlands are vitally important temporary homes. These are the young of certain fish, crabs, and other creatures that spend their earliest days in wetlands before moving on to open waters. The thick vegetation of a wetland is a good place to hide, and the rich food supply gets growing animals off to a healthy start.

Havens for Rare Ones: Wood storks, snail kites, whooping cranes, and American crocodiles are all endangered species—and they all live in wetlands. In fact, about 35 percent of all of the animals and plants listed as threatened or endangered in the United States either live in wetlands or depend on them in some way. That means that more than a third of the nation's rare animals and plants are inseparably linked to areas that, altogether, make up only about five percent of the total land area in the lower 48 states. This fact doesn't seem to leave room for much optimism—especially since wetlands are still being dredged, drained, and filled in for farms, houses, and other developments. But wetlands *are* getting some protection. To find out more about how people are helping to preserve wetlands, see "Taking Care of Wetlands" on page 48.

Create a Scene

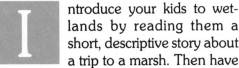

Listen to a description of a wetland and create a wetland scene with picture cut-outs.

Objective:
Identify some of the plants and animals that live in a wetland.

Ages:
Primary

Materials:
- *copies of page 14*
- *crayons or markers*
- *scissors*
- *glue*
- *paper*
- *pictures of wetlands*

Subjects:
Science and Art

Introduce your kids to wetlands by reading them a short, descriptive story about a trip to a marsh. Then have them create their own freshwater marsh scenes to become familiar with the plants and animals that live in a typical marsh.

Start off the activity by explaining what a wetland is and describing some of the different types of wetlands. (See the background information on pages 18-20 and 33-35.) Show pictures of several different types of wetlands that are found in North America. Then pass out copies of page 14 and tell the children that the plants and animals pictured are often found in freshwater marshes—one of the most common types of wetlands. Have them close their eyes and try to imagine what it's like to take a walk in a marsh as you read "In the Marsh" (see the next page).

Ask the children if they have ever explored a place like the one described. Explain that freshwater marshes like this are found all across North America. Now ask the children if they can identify the plants and animals on the Copycat Page (see below). (The names of these plants and animals appear in the story in color.)

Talk a little bit about the plants and animals shown. See if the kids can describe how each one is adapted to living in a wetland habitat. For example, the heron's long legs help it wade in shallow water while it searches for its food. After your discussion, have the kids color in the pictures.

Next pass out a sheet of blank paper to each person. Tell the kids to draw a marsh background scene on the blank paper (see diagram). Then have them cut out their plants and animals and glue them down in their scenes to create a freshwater marsh picture. (Tell the kids to cut out each picture as close to its border as possible.) They can also draw in other marsh plants and/or animals.

If there is a marsh nearby, take the kids on a field trip so they can look for some of the marsh plants and animals they learned about. (For more about visiting wetlands, see "Explore a Wetland" on page 8.)

(continued next page)

bulrushes   great blue heron   Canada geese

red-winged blackbird   frog   mosquito   muskrat   ducks   dragonfly   cattails

5

As you walk out of the forest, you can see a wide open area up ahead. It looks like a grassy meadow that has never been mowed. Off in the distance you can see a patch of open water. Grasses and other plants are growing along the edge and in the open water.

As you walk toward the water, you feel the warmth of the sun beating down on your head and back. The plants are sharp and scratchy as they brush against your skin. Gradually you feel something cool seep into your sneakers. Looking down, you see that your feet are getting soaked.

Squish. Squoosh. Slosh. Sloosh. The ground becomes less firm and the water is now almost up to your ankles. You notice a strange, marshy smell as you slog through the gooey mud.

Suddenly you hear a loud buzz and catch a glimmer of red out of the corner of your eye. It's a dragonfly swooping down to land on a cattail. The dragon-fly's see-through wings glisten in the sunlight. You reach out to gently touch it, but it's too late. The dragonfly has zipped away to hunt for mosquitoes and other marsh insects. Instead of touching the dragonfly, you feel the soft fuzz of the cattail.

A small black bird darts by, flashing its bright red shoulder patches at you and squawking *Ok-ra-leee!* It's a red-winged blackbird. Are you too close to its nest? As quietly as possible you slosh away and continue toward the open water.

The ground is now oozier and the water is deeper. As you bend over to roll up your pant legs, you hear a hum. *Slap!* Too late! You can already feel the tiny sting of a mosquito bite behind your ear. Trying not to scratch it, you move on. *Squish, slosh, squish. Plop!* What was that? Could it be a frog? Or maybe a muskrat? Whatever made the noise escapes quickly and quietly through the maze of cattail stalks.

Up ahead, you spy several ducks paddling silently across the water. As you creep up to get a better look, you realize the water is almost up to your knees. You decide it's time to turn around and head back to dry land.

As you retrace your steps, you can hear the loud, honking sounds of Canada geese flying in the distance. And you see a great blue heron flying gracefully overhead. It has long, steel-blue wings and a slender, S-shaped neck. And its long legs trail behind it like the tail of a kite. The heron circles and lands on the opposite edge of the water near some tall bulrushes. It wades easily through the water, stretching its neck out as it searches for a meal. Then it pauses for a moment and stands motionless. Suddenly, with a quick dip of its head, it grabs a small fish.

Finally you're back on dry land. As you think about everything you saw and felt, you realize the marsh is a very special place.

Surveys and Slogans

Take a wetland survey and design a wetland stamp, poster, T-shirt, or bumper sticker.

Objectives:
Describe several animals that depend on wetlands. List an endangered species that lives in a wetland.

Ages:
Intermediate

Hundreds of species of plants and animals depend on wetlands for food, water, and shelter, and as a place to raise their young. By making posters, T-shirts, stamps, and/or bumper stickers your kids can let others know that wetlands are valuable wildlife habitats.

Before starting the activity, write the four questions on the next page on a piece of paper, leaving space for answers between the questions. Make enough copies so that each person can get four copies of the survey.

CRABS ARE COOL

SAVE OUR WETLANDS

Materials:
- markers, crayons, or poster paints
- copies of the questions provided in the activity
- cardboard
- scissors
- glue
- reference books

Subjects:
Science and Art

WETLAND QUESTIONNAIRE

1. Is there a swamp, bog, freshwater marsh, salt marsh, or other type of wetland in or near your community? If so, describe it.

2. Can you list several reasons why wetlands are important?

3. Can you name several animals that depend on wetlands?

4. Can you name two famous wetlands in North America?

Pass out one copy of the survey to each person in the group and have the kids answer each question as best they can. To get them started, talk about the characteristics of a wetland (see the background information on pages 3-4). Freshwater marshes and swamps, bogs, salt marshes, and mangrove swamps are all types of wetlands.

Afterward, collect the papers and explain that you will be discussing the answers later. Then pass out three more copies of the page to each person. Tell the kids that they should try to find three adults who are willing to fill out the survey. Give the children several days to get their surveys completed, then discuss the answers using the background information on pages 3-4. Ask the group if most of the people that they surveyed were familiar with wetlands. Have them describe some of the local wetlands that were mentioned on the surveys. Then ask them to list some of the better-known wetlands in North America. (For more about North American wetlands, see "Put It on the Map!" on page 12.) Finally, talk about how wetlands are important to wildlife. List some of the animals that depend on wetlands, including endangered, threatened, and rare species (see questions 2 and 18 on page 54).

Now tell the group that each person is going to get a chance to tell others about the importance of wetlands by designing a wetland stamp, poster, T-shirt, or bumper sticker. Explain that their creations should include a catchy slogan, as well as a design or picture that symbolizes a way that wetlands are important to wildlife. (See the drawings for some examples of slogans and pictures.) Each person can focus on a specific type of wetland or come up with a general wetland theme. Give the kids research time to find out more about the plants and animals that live in the types of wetlands they chose.

Afterward, display the finished wetland posters, T-shirts, stamps, and bumper stickers so that other people can learn more about why wetlands are important. You can also hold a contest to see which designs and slogans are the favorites.

*Take a walk in a wet-
land and then make a
wetland picture story or
fill in a wetland work-
sheet.*

Objectives:
*Name several wetland
animals and plants.
Discuss some wetland
safety tips.*

Ages:
*Primary, Intermediate,
and Advanced*

Materials:
- *pictures of wetlands*
- *copies of page 15*
- *crayons or markers*
- *pencils*
- *scissors*
- *glue*
- *paper*
- *field guides (see
suggestions in activity
and in bibliography)*
- *clipboards or
cardboard and rubber
bands*
- *white baking dishes,
bowls, or collecting
pans for observing
creatures (optional)*
- *thermometer, wind
gauge, or other
weather equipment
(optional)*
- *hand lenses
(optional)*
- *"Romp in the
Swamp" album by Bill
Brennan (optional)*

Subjects:
*Science and Creative
Writing*

T ake your kids on a wetland safari so they can get a firsthand look at a unique, watery community. We've provided a couple of different activity options you can try, depending on the age group you're working with. (You might also want to combine parts of both activities.)

Before setting out on an expedition with your group, visit the wetland yourself to become familiar with its features and wildlife. Also take a look at the "Tips for Wetland Wanderers" at the end of the activity. Go over the safety suggestions with the kids—then get them outside and into the wild world of wetlands!

OPTION #1: SAY IT WITH PICTURES (FOR YOUNGER KIDS)

On the day of your wetland trip, show the kids pictures of the kind of wetland they'll be visiting. (See the background information on pages 18-20 and pages 33-35 for information about the different kinds of wetlands.) You might also want to play some songs from Bill Brennan's album entitled "Romp in the Swamp" to help get the kids in a "wetland mood." We've included information about how to order the album on page 64.

When you get to the wetland, try some of the following activities:
- Have the kids make a list of the different kinds and numbers of animals they see. (Even though they may see a lot of the larger animals, such as birds, remind them that there are many smaller animals living among the wetland plants and in the soil.)
- Let the kids look at a sample of wetland soil with hand lenses. (If you visit a bog, look at the sphagnum moss.) Can you see any insects or other small animals moving around in it?
- Keep an eye out for animal signs. For example, you might come across some animal tracks or droppings. Or you might discover a bird nest or the lodge of a beaver or muskrat.
- Take the group into a non-wetland area (forest, field, or prairie) that's near the wetland you're visiting. Can they see any plants and animals that are different from those in the wetland?

When you get back to the classroom or nature center, pass out copies of page 15. Explain that each person will be writing a paragraph or two about the wetland they

visited, using pictures from page 15 that they've colored, cut out, and glued down. For example, a description of a trip to a swamp could start off this way:

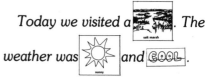

Today we visited a ____. The weather was ____ and ____.

For best results the kids should color the pictures they want to use before they cut them out and glue them down. They might want to add a few original pictures too. Tell them that just about anything goes, and encourage them to use their imaginations. (How about a fantasy story about the wetland? Or an account of life in the wetland from an animal's point of view?) No matter what approach they take, they should include the following information in their paragraphs:
- the name and a picture of at least one plant they saw on their visit
- the names and pictures of three or more animals they saw on their visit
- a description and a picture of at least one animal sign they came across

When all of the groups are finished, talk about the pictures from page 15 that each person used. The pictures they chose will probably vary enough to give a good representation of the different things the kids saw on their wetland excursion.

Here's a way to help your kids key in on the variety and diversity of a wetland community. Before visiting a wetland, tell the kids to pretend that they're wildlife biologists who have been hired by the state to survey the plant and animal life of the wetland you'll be visiting. The state has come up with a list of information it wants the biologists to determine. Here's a sample of the kinds of things the biologists might be asked to find out:

- the dominant plant species
- the names of other kinds of plants growing in the wetland
- a description of the soil and the creatures that live there (Do insects live in the soil? crustaceans? mollusks? what else?)
- weather conditions (temperature of the air and/or soil, wind speed and direction, percent cloud cover, and so on)
- the names of several species of birds seen in the wetland, and a description of what they were doing (flying, feeding, preening, and so on)
- the names of at least two species of insects seen in the wetland, and a description of what they were doing (flying, sunning, biting, and so on)
- the names of other animals seen in the wetland, and a description of what they were doing

- a description of any animal signs seen in the wetland (tracks, droppings, nests, lodges, burrows, and so on)
- the total number of each species of animals identified
- a comparison of plants and animals of the wetland with those of a nearby, non-wetland habitat
- the temperature of the air several feet above the ground compared to the temperature at ground level

You can either modify the above suggestions into worksheet questions that the kids can answer at the wetland, or you can come up with a chart that they can fill in during their visit. (See the example.) You might even want to have the kids come up with their own charts, as a field biologist might do. On the backs of their charts, they could jot down any information that doesn't fit on the chart, such as the descriptions of soil and weather conditions.

When you get to the wetland, you might want to pass out field guides for the kids to use. (The Golden Nature Guide entitled *Pond Life* and Delta Education's *OBIS Pond Guide* are two good ones for freshwater wetlands. You might want to bring bird and insect field guides too. See the bibliography for suggestions of some other field guides you can use.) Also pass out clipboards for the kids' worksheets or charts. (If you don't have clipboards, have the kids attach their sheets to cardboard with rubber bands.)

After the wetland visit, talk about all the things the kids saw. Explain that real wildlife biologists who are hired to do surveys of an area make many trips into the area to get a good indication of the plants and animals that live there. One trip usually can't reveal all of the life an area harbors. So there's probably a lot more to the wetland your group visited than they discovered while taking their surveys. You might want to try visiting the wetland at least one more time—maybe during a different season. *(continued next page)*

SAMPLE CHART

SURVEY OF THE SALISBURY SALT MARSH			
Plants	**Animals**		
	Birds	**Insects**	**Miscellaneous**

spartina (dominant)
glasswort
phragmites
groundsel
	great blue herons IIII
	snowy egrets III
	bald eagles I
	clapper rails
	   heard IIII
	   saw none
		dragonflies
		damselflies
		mosquitoes
		grasshoppers
		deer flies
			whitetail deer III
			raccoon—*tracks seen*
			snails—*everywhere*

- **Bring along "bug" juice**—Where there's a wetland, there are usually insects—especially on warm or hot days with no wind. (Biting insects tend to "lie low" on cool, windy days.) You can discourage mosquitoes and other biting insects by wearing long pants and long-sleeved shirts. And be sure to have some insect repellent on hand!

- **Stay on the boardwalk**—Try to visit a park or reserve that has a boardwalk extending into the wetland area. A boardwalk can prevent a muddy hike—and it protects fragile plants and small animals.

- **How about a boat?**—Consider taking a canoe through the tidal creeks of a salt marsh, around the cypress "knees" in a swamp, or just offshore from some tangled mangrove thickets. You may be able to get closer to wildlife this way (you can often approach more quietly on the water), and you'll be able to see fish and other aquatic life.

- **Be prepared to get your feet wet**—This holds true for any wetland you may visit, particularly if it doesn't have a boardwalk. Old sneakers can be good wetland shoes—but if you step into a really soggy or muddy area, walk carefully. (It's easy to lose sneakers in the muck! Old boots are more likely to stay on your feet.) You might want to tell the kids to bring extra shoes and socks that they can change into later.

- **Remember the first aid kit**—Just in case! It's also a good idea to carry some food and water, even on short trips.

- **Take only memories**—Remind the kids not to pick plants or take animals from the wetland. Certain plants or animals that seem common in the wetland you're visiting may be very rare everywhere else. Some may even be endangered. It's against the law to collect endangered species without a special permit, and in many states, it's against the law to collect any species from parks or refuges.

- **Don't go poking around!**—Tell the kids not to put fingers under rocks, logs, or in other hidden-from-view places. As with almost any habitat, some wetlands are home to critters that bite or sting—and a few of these animals are poisonous. Such animals often live or hide in secluded places.

- **Try a winter walk**—Don't rule out winter as a time to visit wetlands—particularly marshes. If the ground is frozen it can be much easier to walk on. (Tell the kids to wear shoes or boots with slip-resistant soles, though, just in case you come across any icy spots.) And insects usually aren't a problem in winter, since most die or go into hibernation when the weather gets cold.

snowy egret and young

Leonard Lee Rue III

Wetland Models

Make a clay model of a wetland and discover how a wetland works.

Objectives:
Discuss what a wetland is. Describe several functions of a wetland.

Ages:
Intermediate and Advanced

Materials:
- *chalkboard or easel paper*
- *modeling clay*
- *Oasis (florist foam)*
- *roasting pans*
- *small piece of indoor-outdoor carpeting*
- *sponges*
- *pine needles, twigs, grass, weeds, soil, and other natural materials*
- *cotton swabs (optional)*
- *toothpicks (optional)*
- *cardboard*
- *glue*
- *scissors*
- *paper and pencils*
- *crayons or markers*
- *pictures of wetlands and wetland plants and animals*
- *jar of muddy water*
- *water*
- *reference books*
- *poster paints*

Subject:
Science

It's hard to tell, just by looking at wetlands, that they help filter silt and pollutants from water, help prevent soil erosion, and often reduce flood damage. But by building a simplified wetland model, you can demonstrate some of these important wetland functions.

Before you begin the activity, make a demonstration model. Here's how to do it:

1. Spread a layer of modeling clay in half of the roasting pan to represent land. Leave the other half of the pan empty to represent a lake or other body of water, such as a river or ocean.
2. Shape the clay so that it gradually slopes down to the body of water (see diagram).

3. Smooth the clay along the sides of the pan to seal the edges. You can also form meandering streams in the clay that lead into the body of water.
4. Cut a piece of indoor-outdoor carpeting to completely fill the space across the pan along the edge of the clay (see diagram). The carpeting represents the wetland buffer between dry land and open water.

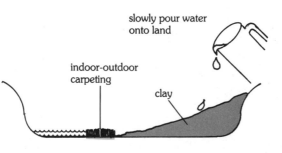

Begin the activity by asking the kids to list the characteristics of a wetland. Write their answers on a chalkboard or large sheet of easel paper. Take a group survey to decide which of the characteristics might apply to all wetlands. (See the background information on pages 3-4.)

Next show the group some pictures of different types of wetlands, including freshwater and salt marshes, freshwater swamps, mangrove swamps, and bogs. Have the kids think about the animals and plants that might live in each kind of wetland. (For examples, see the background information on pages 18-20 and 33-35.)

Now demonstrate some of the functions of a wetland using the model. Explain that wetlands, like all habitats, are very complicated natural systems. And scientists are still learning more about how they work. Scientists already know that wetlands perform some very important functions, such as filtering pollutants, reducing flood damage, and preventing soil erosion. (Scientists also think that some wetlands, at times, might help to recharge underground water supplies.) Explain that your model will demonstrate some of these functions in a very simplified way. Here are a couple of the functions you can demonstrate with the model:

Flood Control: Fit the piece of carpeting into the wetland area. Pour some water slowly on the land, as shown. Have the kids describe what happens. (Some of the water is slowed down by the wetland [carpeting]. The excess slowly flows into the body of water.)

Now remove the carpeting and water. This time pour the same amount of water on the model at the same spot and rate as before. Have the kids note any differences. (The water should fill the body of water much more quickly than before. That's because it's no longer buffered by the wetland. Explain that most wetlands are shallow basins that collect water and slow its rate of flow. This slowing process helps reduce flooding and also helps prevent soil erosion.)

In many coastal areas wetlands are drained and filled in, and houses or marinas are built right along the water. Without a wetland buffer, these developed areas are often subjected to severe flooding and erosion, especially during violent storms.

Water Purification: Pour the water out of the model and replace the piece of carpeting in the wetland. Pour some muddy water from the jar onto the land. Ask the kids to compare the water that ends up in the body of water with the water in the jar. (Explain that the soil particles are trapped by the carpeting, making the water in the body of water much clearer.)

Remove the carpeting, pour out the water, and try the experiment again. What happens without the wetland in place? Ask the kids why all the dirt particles end up in the body of water now. (The thick mat of plant roots in a wetland helps trap silt and some types of pollutants. Without a wetland, excessive amounts of silt and pollutants can end up in lakes, rivers, and other bodies of water. See "Silt Trappers"

on page 4 to find out more about how wetlands act as natural filters.)

After demonstrating some wetland functions, discuss how wetlands are important wildlife habitats, as well as important recreation sites for people. (See the background information on pages 46-48 for more about how wetlands are important to people and wildlife.)

Now divide your group into smaller groups of about five each. Tell each group they will be making their own wetland models out of clay, using your model as an example. (Instead of using indoor-outdoor carpeting to represent a wetland, have them use Oasis [florist foam] molded into a very shallow basin. Then the kids can attach plants and animals to the model with toothpicks.) They can make a freshwater marsh, a salt marsh, a freshwater swamp, a mangrove swamp, or a bog. Provide reference books so the kids can see pictures of the different types of wetlands. Then have them decorate the models according to the types of wetlands they are making. Here are some ideas:

- For cattails, use cotton swabs painted brown, pieces of grass, or toothpicks painted green with bits of brown clay stuck on the tops.
- Use long pine needles for reeds.
- Shape wetland creatures from clay or cut them from paper and glue onto toothpicks.
- Make trees by gluing pieces of green sponge onto twigs.

Put It on the Map!

Use clues to identify the locations of some major North American wetlands.

Objectives:
Name several major wetlands. Describe an important feature about each one and locate it on a map.

Ages:
Advanced

Here's a challenging way to help your group become familiar with some of our major wetlands. Start by discussing what wetlands are and the kinds of places where they occur. (See the background information on pages 3-4.) Explain that there are a number of significant wetlands in North America. Some are significant because they are extensive and provide important wildlife habitat. Some are homes to rare plants and animals. Some provide important resources for people. And some have historical and

cultural value. Tell your group that they will discover what some of these major wetlands are and where they're located.

Then pass out copies of page 16 and 17. Explain that each wetland is marked on the map with a code that symbolizes a particular type of wetland (freshwater marsh, salt marsh, swamp, or bog). The goal is to identify each of the wetlands by name on the line under each clue on page 16, to identify each wetland by letter on the lines on the map, and then to identify which kind of wetland each code symbolizes.

Materials:
- *copies of pages 16 and 17*
- *reference books*
- *large sheets of construction paper (optional)*
- *glue (optional)*
- *scissors (optional)*
- *colored yarn (optional)*
- *world map*

Subjects:
Science and Geography

Give the kids research time to discover which wetland, geographic region, body of water, or city or state each clue is referring to. You can have them work individually or in teams. If they work together, you might want to add a little extra challenge by having the teams try to be the first to identify all the wetlands on the map and label the key correctly.

Each team could also make a poster out of the map. Here's how:
1. Glue the map onto a large sheet of construction paper.
2. Cut out the clues and glue them around the border of the paper.
3. Use pieces of colored yarn to connect the clues with the proper wetlands on the map (see diagram below).

BRANCHING OUT: WHERE IN THE WORLD?

Have the kids bone up on their geography skills by learning about some significant wetlands around the globe. Use the following information to discuss a few of these special areas. Then have the kids try to point out the countries where these wetlands are located on a world map.

Tigris-Euphrates: This marshy middle eastern river valley was the world's "cradle of civilization" and is still home to a group of people called the Marsh Arabs. These people of southern Iraq have found many uses for the reeds that grow near their marshy villages, such as a source of building material for houses and boats, and as sources of fuel and cattle feed.

Tollund Bog: In 1950, peat miners discovered a perfectly preserved, 2000-year-old body of a man in this Danish bog. The acids in this type of wetland inhibited the process of decay so that even the whiskers on the man's chin were intact.

Pantanal: South America's most important waterfowl habitat is a floodplain wetland. (Floodplain wetlands form along rivers and are subjected to periodic floodings.) The Pantanal stretches across 20 million acres (8 million ha), most of which are in Brazil. This wild wetland is home to such creatures as howler monkeys, capybaras, caimans, and jabiru storks.

Finland: Wetlands cover almost one-third of this Scandinavian country. In fact, its name comes from a word for a type of wetland—"fen."

Orinoco Delta: Mangrove swamps line the shores of this area of Venezuela. When people attempted to drain the Orinoco Delta for agriculture, they created desertlike conditions.

Sudd: The extensive marshes of this Nile River floodplain in South Sudan are important to waterfowl migrating from Europe to Africa. Many other animals, including people, also depend on these marshes for fish and other foods.

Wadden Sea: This region is the largest wetland in the Netherlands. It has been drastically reduced since dikes were first built about 2000 years ago.

Answers: 1—Nebraska (L); 2—Prairie Pothole Region (A); 3—Minnesota (F); 4—Great Swamp (G); 5—Boston (H); 6—Pine Barrens (K); 7—Chesapeake Bay (D); 8—Dismal Swamp (N); 9—Four Holes Swamp (J); 10—Okefenokee (O); 11—Everglades (E); 12—Atchafalaya (C); 13—Big Thicket (P); 14—Alakai (B); 15—Yukon Flats (I); 16—San Francisco Bay (M)

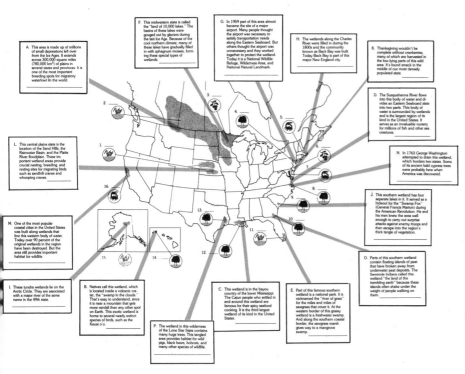

SYMBOLS KEY

Freshwater Marsh

Swamp

Bog

Salt Marsh

cloudy

animal tracks

mosquito

dragonfly

mangroves

sphagnum moss

freshwater swamp

raccoon

COLD

COOL

cattails

rushes

muskrat or beaver lodge

fiddler crabs

muskrat

wading birds

salt marsh

deer

freshwater marsh

snails

WINDY

CALM

pitcher plant

sundew

clams

mussels

geese

ducks

hawk

mangrove swamp

frogs

sunny

HOT

WARM

trees

grasses

beaver

bog

fish

RANGER RICK'S NATURESCOPE: WADING INTO WETLANDS

A. This area is made up of millions of small depressions left over from the Ice Ages. It extends across 300,000 square miles (780,000 km^2) of plains in several states and provinces. It is one of the most important breeding spots for migratory waterfowl in the world.

_____

B. Natives call this wetland, which is located inside a volcanic crater, the "swamp in the clouds." That's easy to understand, since it is near a mountain that gets more rainfall than any other spot on Earth. This exotic wetland is home to several nearly extinct species of birds, such as the Kauai o'o.

_____

C. This wetland is in the bayou country of the lower Mississippi. The Cajun people who settled in and around this wetland are famous for their spicy seafood cooking. It is the third largest wetland of its kind in the United States.

_____

D. The Susquehanna River flows into this body of water and divides an Eastern Seaboard state into two parts. This body of water is surrounded by wetlands and is the largest region of its kind in the United States. It serves as an invaluable nursery for millions of fish and other sea creatures.

_____

E. Part of this famous southern wetland is a national park. It is nicknamed the "river of grass" for the miles and miles of sawgrass that cover it. At the western border of this grassy wetland is a freshwater swamp. And along the southern coastal border, the sawgrass marsh gives way to a mangrove swamp.

_____

F. This midwestern state is called the "land of 10,000 lakes." The basins of these lakes were gouged out by glaciers during the last Ice Age. Because of the cool northern climate, many of these lakes have gradually filled in with sphagnum mosses, forming these special types of wetlands.

_____

G. In 1959 part of this area almost became the site of a major airport. Many people thought the airport was necessary to satisfy transportation needs along the Eastern Seaboard. But others thought the airport was unnecessary and they worked together to protect the wetland. Today it is a National Wildlife Refuge, Wilderness Area, and National Natural Landmark.

_____

H. The wetlands along the Charles River were filled in during the 1800s and the community known as Back Bay was built. Today Back Bay is part of this major New England city.

_____

I. These tundra wetlands lie on the Arctic Circle. They are associated with a major river of the same name in the 49th state.

_____

J. This southern wetland has four separate lakes in it. It served as a hideout for the "Swamp Fox" (General Francis Marion) during the American Revolution. He and his men knew the area well enough to carry out surprise attacks against enemy troops and then escape into the region's thick tangle of vegetation.

_____

Alakai	Yukon Flats
Boston	Pine Barrens
Nebraska	Atchafalaya
Minnesota	Dismal Swamp
Okefenokee	Chesapeake Bay
Everglades	Four Holes Swamp
Great Swamp	San Francisco Bay
Big Thicket	Prairie Pothole Region

K. Thanksgiving wouldn't be complete without cranberries, many of which are harvested in the low-lying parts of this wild area. It's found smack in the middle of our most densely populated state.

_____

L. This central plains state is the location of the Sand Hills, the Rainwater Basin, and the Platte River floodplain. These important wetland areas provide crucial nesting, breeding, and resting sites for migrating birds such as sandhill cranes and whooping cranes.

_____

M. One of the most popular coastal cities in the United States was built along wetlands that line this western body of water. Today over 80 percent of the original wetlands in the region have been destroyed. But the area still provides important habitat for wildlife.

_____

N. In 1763 George Washington attempted to drain this wetland, which borders two states. Some of its ancient bald cypress trees were probably here when America was discovered.

_____

O. Parts of this southern wetland contain floating islands of peat that have broken away from underwater peat deposits. The Seminole Indians called this wetland "the land of the trembling earth" because these islands often shake under the weight of people walking on them.

_____

P. The wetland in this wilderness of the Lone Star State contains many huge trees. This tangled area provides habitat for wild pigs, black bears, bobcats, and many other species of wildlife.

_____

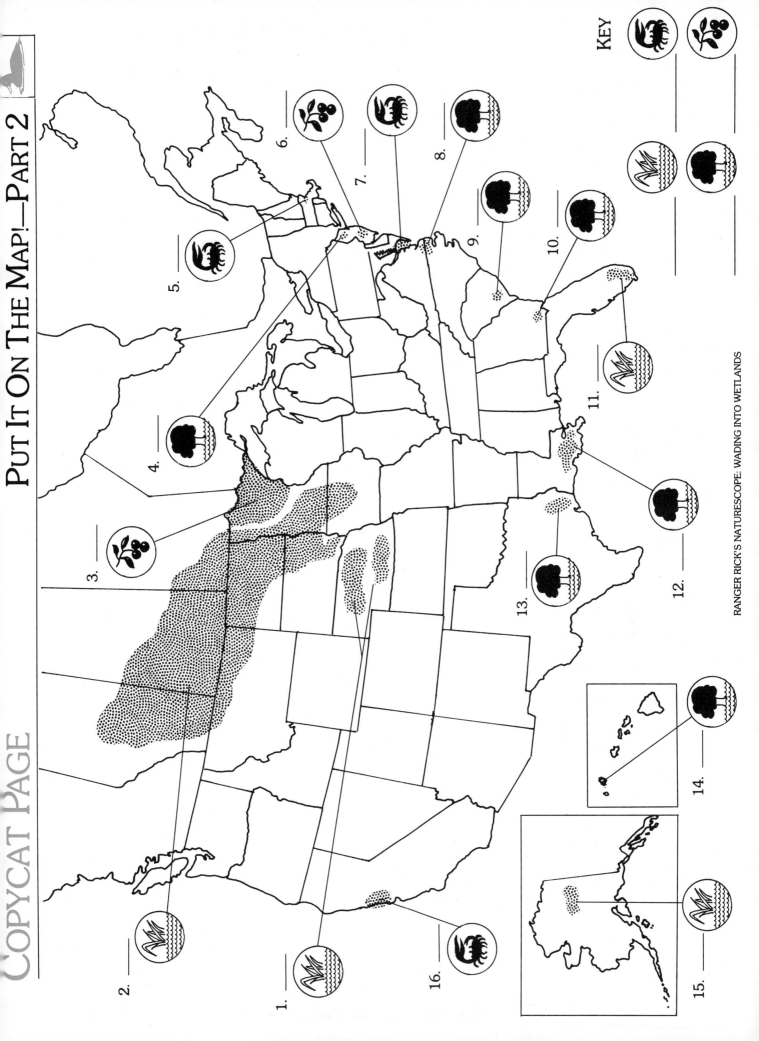

COPYCAT PAGE

PUT IT ON THE MAP!—PART 2

KEY

RANGER RICK'S NATURESCOPE: WADING INTO WETLANDS

SALTWATER WETLANDS

Stretching along much of the world's coastlines are ribbons of life—productive and important communities of plants and animals that flourish between the open waters of the oceans and the dry lands beyond. These communities, the saltwater wetlands, take several different forms. In the tropics, for example, they're mangrove swamps: thick stands of mangrove trees and the host of organisms that live among their tangled roots and branches. But north and south of the tropics, in the temperate zones, mangrove swamps give way to the open, grassy wetlands called salt marshes. Both of these major kinds of saltwater wetlands support rich networks of life adapted to dynamic, often unpredictable, environments.

IN TUNE WITH THE TIDES

Mangrove swamps and salt marshes are different in a lot of ways—mainly because they occur in different climates. But they're alike in that they're both subjected to some of the same kinds of conditions, day in and day out. These conditions are dictated by a powerful force: the oceans' tides.

Daily Ups and Downs: Twice each day along most of the world's coasts, the tide rises and falls. What this daily fluctuation in the water level means to saltwater wetlands is that they're exposed to a continually changing environment. For part of the day mangrove swamps and salt marshes are flooded, and many of the plants and animals that live in them become partially or completely covered with water. Then, as the tide gradually retreats, the plants and animals become exposed to air.

It's not just the water level that changes, though. So does the temperature of the wetland—each time the tide comes and goes. (In warm seasons water tends to be cooler than air or land, and in cool seasons it's often warmer.) Rising and falling tides also bring increases and decreases in the salt content, or *salinity,* of a coastal wetland. (For some examples of how certain salt marsh and mangrove swamp plants and animals have adapted to their habitats, see "Amazing Mangroves" on page 22 and "Changing with the Tide" on page 27.)

Molding Marshes; Shaping Swamps: Changes in a saltwater wetland aren't limited to the tides' ups and downs and the increases and decreases in temperature and salinity that they bring. Over time, the whole wetland changes—shifting, shrinking, or expanding depending on factors such as weather patterns and climatic changes. For example, a single violent storm can wash away part of a wetland or create areas where new wetlands can take hold. (Sediment washed up on shores can make fertile ground for wetland plants.) Gradual changes in the sea level can also affect wetlands. As the sea level rises, a new wetland can form where, say, a forest once stood. And as the sea level falls, fields, forests, and other "dry" habitats can eventually develop in a former wetland.

SALTWATER WETLANDS UP CLOSE

Here's a closer look at salt marshes and mangrove swamps, starting with the most abundant and widely distributed of the two.

SALT MARSHES

Seaside "Prairies": In a way, salt marshes are the prairies of the coasts. A sea of grasses characterizes these wetlands, which in the United States are most extensive between the coasts of southern Massachusetts and northern Florida. But these

saltwater "prairies" have a different look from, for example, the prairies of the American Midwest. One reason for this is that they're intersected here and there by *tidal creeks*—saltwater creeks that rise and fall with the tides.

A Dirty Build-Up: Salt marshes are a common feature of the world's coasts, but they don't occur along just any type of shore. The inner reaches of coves, inlets, estuaries, and bays make some of the best sites for salt marshes, since they're protected from the full force of the pounding surf. Sediment brought in on the tides and nutrient-rich silt carried in by rivers can settle in these calmer areas, giving marsh plants an ideal place to sprout, grow, and spread. Once they've gotten started, the plants trap even more sediments and silt among their roots and around their stems. And when they die, their leaves, stems, and roots become part of the sediment too, making the soil richer for future generations of plants.

Impressive Producers: Grasses are the most common plants in many salt marshes, and usually only one or two grass species dominate the scene. These grasses are often members of the tough, productive group known as the spartinas.

Spartina grasses are the bread and butter of many salt marshes. These grasses are incredible producers, creating as much or more food per acre than most carefully cultivated and heavily fertilized agricultural fields of the same size. All of the animals in a spartina salt marsh depend on this "generous" food source, either directly or indirectly. (In western salt marshes, pickelweeds, spike grasses, and certain other plants are often more abundant than spartina.)

Webs of Life: The bacteria of a salt marsh contribute a lot to the marsh plants' ability to feed so many. Through the process of decomposition, they break down the dead stems and leaves of spartina and other plants into a form that other animals can use. (Only certain insects, crabs, and a few other animals can digest the tough plants in their original form.) This decomposed vegetation, along with tiny bits of animal remains and other "scraps," is known collectively as *detritus.* Salt marsh algae grow on detritus, and crabs, fish, mussels, clams, and many other animals feed on these enriched bits of food. The detritus eaters eventually become food for birds and other marsh predators. (Detritus also "feeds" the plants of a salt marsh.)

Tiny as they are, these detritus particles can be important far beyond the boundaries of the salt marsh. Some detritus washes out to sea on the tides where, either directly or indirectly, it may feed ocean animals.

The Smaller the Better: Because of all the food salt marshes have to offer, they support a lot of life—more than most forests, oceans, prairies, and other types of habitats of equal size. But many salt marsh organisms are small or even microscopic. Salt marsh mud, for example, is alive with billions of bacteria and other tiny organisms. And insects, snails, mussels, crabs, and others live in and around the mud, within the tidal creeks, or among the marsh grasses and other plants.

Not many larger animals make the salt marsh their permanent home, though. Some animals, such as raccoons, foxes, and minks, use the marshes as hunting grounds. And big browsers such as deer often come into the marshes too, to feed on the grasses and other plants.

Migrating birds and the young of certain species of animals are two other groups of salt marsh "part-timers." For more about how they use salt marshes and other wetlands, see "Migration Vacations" and "Natural Nurseries" on page 4.

(continued next page)

Bill Weber

Between Marsh and Sea: Special habitats called tidal flats often border the seaward edges of salt marshes. Tidal flats are muddy (and/or sandy) areas that lie exposed during low tide and become completely inundated with water during high tide. Most plants—including the hardy spartinas—don't grow in these severe conditions. As a result, tidal flats look pretty barren at first glance.

But there's more to tidal flats than you might think. Algae and bacteria are incredibly abundant in these areas, and they provide food for the clams, crabs, snails, worms, and many other small animals that live in the mud. During low tide, sandpipers and many other birds "flock" to the exposed flats to gobble up these animals. And during high tide, fish and other animals swim into the flats to feed.

MANGROVE SWAMPS

Where the Salt Marshes End: Mangrove swamps are the tropical counterparts to the salt marshes of cooler climates. As in salt marshes, the mangrove swamp community depends on a group of related plants that produce huge quantities of food and provide homes for many different kinds of animals. But the dominant plants of mangrove swamps are mangrove trees, not grasses or other non-woody plants.

Frost can kill mangrove trees, which is why the swamp communities they support occur mainly in the tropics. In the United States mangrove swamps reach their most lush growth along the coasts of southern Florida, although a few small stands of mangroves straggle as far north as coastal Louisiana and Texas.

Living Stilts and Sticks in the Mud: The special habitat most mangroves grow in calls for some special adjustments. For one thing, coasts don't make for very stable growing conditions. Also, mangrove swamp mud doesn't have much oxygen in it. The multitudes of bacteria and other tiny organisms that live in the mud quickly use up oxygen in the process of decomposition.

The roots of certain species of mangroves have evolved some interesting solutions to these problems. For example, red mangroves send out *prop roots:* long roots that grow down from their trunks and branches and become anchored in the mud. These stiltlike roots trap leaves, detritus, and other floating debris, making the trees' footing firmer. Prop roots also absorb oxygen from the air through tiny pores called *lenticels.*

Black mangroves don't need as much support as red mangroves do, so they don't have prop roots. (Black mangroves grow on slightly firmer ground than red mangroves. And they usually aren't exposed to as much wave action, since they grow a little farther inland.) Like red mangroves, though, black mangroves are faced with the problem of low oxygen levels in the soil. They cope with this situation by sending up small, sticklike roots from the mud. These roots, called *pneumatophores,* are covered with lenticels, just as a red mangrove's prop roots are.

"No One Likes the Mangroves...": Author John Steinbeck wrote these words—and at the time he was right. Nearly everybody once thought of mangroves as useless, weedy "junk" trees. Now we realize that there's plenty to like about mangroves and the mangrove swamp communities. For example, they're great storm breakers. And their jungle of roots and dense leaves and branches makes them popular places for wildlife. Some animals—certain kinds of oysters, for example—cling to mangrove roots. Others, such as shrimp, fish, and crabs, hide and feed among the roots submerged by high tide. And in the mangrove branches overhead, storks, herons, egrets, and hundreds of other species of birds nest and roost. To these animals and many others, mangroves are anything but "junk" trees. (For more about the wildlife of mangrove swamps, see "Amazing Mangroves" on page 22.)

Make a Mud Snail

Objectives:
Name and describe several of the body parts of a mud snail. Talk about some of the adaptations that help a mud snail survive in its habitat.

Ages:
Primary

Materials:
- *copies of page 30*
- *pictures of mud snails*
- *scissors*
- *construction paper or drawing paper*
- *glue*
- *crayons or markers*

Subject:
Science

ere's a fun way for the kids in your group to get a close-up look at one saltwater wetland creature—the mud snail. Before you get started, make your own mud snail by following the directions below. Then begin by discussing the characteristics and kinds of saltwater wetlands. (See the background information on pages 18-20). Next, tell the kids that you're going to talk about an animal that lives in many coastal areas, including tidal flats and salt marshes. Read them these clues and see if they can guess what kind of creature it might be.

- It eats mostly plants but also dead animals such as fish and crabs.

MAKING A MUD SNAIL

1. Cut out each of the puzzle pieces along the solid lines.
2. Arrange the puzzle pieces to form a picture of a mud snail. Then glue each piece in place on a sheet of construction paper or drawing paper and let dry.
3. Color the snail and label its body parts.

- It has a head, two tentacles, and one "foot."
- It carries its "house" on its "back."
- Its "house" has a "door" that the animal carries around on its foot.
- Its teeth and mouth are on the end of a long, trunklike tube.

After the kids have made their guesses, show them pictures of mud snails. Then, using the mud snail puzzle that you made earlier and the information below, discuss the parts of a mud snail. Afterward pass out copies of page 30, scissors, glue, crayons or markers, and construction paper or drawing paper and let the kids make their own mud snails.

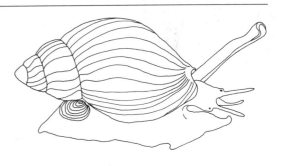

MUD SNAIL SPECIFICS

Mud snails live along the mud banks and in the muddy tidal creeks of salt marshes, as well as in other coastal areas. Like many snails, mud snails need to stay moist. So when the tide goes out, they often "follow the water" or crawl into pools. If a mud snail does get left "high and dry" and starts to get too hot or too dry, it can burrow down into the surface of the mud to stay moist and cool until the tide returns. Here's a look at the parts of a mud snail:

Shell—A mud snail's shell can be a little over one inch (2.5 cm) long and is usually light brown to black. The shell, like the shell of other

snails, is the mud snail's shelter and helps protect it from drying out as well as from some predators. The mud snail can pull its entire body into its shell.

Operculum—The operculum is a horny disc that rides on the back of a mud snail's foot. When a mud snail pulls its body into its shell the operculum comes last, shutting like a door to seal the mud snail inside. When closed, the operculum helps protect a mud snail from some predators and from drying out.

Foot—Mud snails glide from place to place along a single foot. (A snail's foot is the fleshy part of the body that helps the animal move.) As

they move along the mud the foot produces a special slime that makes the gliding easier. Chemicals in this slime can be "read" by other snails and thus aid in communication among individuals.

Proboscis—At the tip of this trunklike tube are the mud snail's teeth and its mouth. The mud snail uses its teeth to scrape algae and other food from the surface of the mud and to scrape flesh from the bodies of dead animals that it finds. As the food is scraped off it goes into the mud snail's mouth.

Siphon—Mud snails' siphons draw water into their bodies and around their gills, which absorb oxygen and give off

carbon dioxide. The water pulled in by the siphon also circulates through a special organ inside the snail's body. This organ can detect chemicals in the water. (Chemicals in the water help a mud snail find food and detect predators. They also aid in communication among individuals.)

Tentacles—A mud snail uses its two tentacles to feel things in front of it and to detect chemicals in the water.

Eyes—The two tiny eyes near the bases of a mud snail's tentacles can't see images the way human eyes do. Instead they detect differences in the amount of light.

Amazing Mangroves

Answer questions about a mangrove swamp scene and sing a song about mangrove communities.

Objectives:
Describe some of the animals that live in a mangrove swamp. Explain the ways these animals use mangrove trees.

Ages:
Primary

Materials:
- *copies of page 31*
- *crayons or markers*
- *guitar or piano (optional)*

Subjects:
Science and Music

Luise Woelflein

 ere's a way to introduce your kids to the mangrove swamp community. First pass out copies of page 31. As the kids look at the scene, discuss some of the ways mangrove trees are adapted to living in coastal waters. (See "Living Stilts and Sticks in the Mud" on page 20.) Tell the kids that the two trees illustrated are red mangroves. Then talk about each of the animals that live on or around the trees using the background information in "Who's Who in the Mangrove" on page 23. Here are some sample questions to ask:

1. How many crabs are there in the picture? Where are they? Do you think they eat the same things?
2. How many birds are there in the picture? Can you name two of the things they are doing?
3. Can you see a snake in the picture? What do you think it's trying to do?
4. Where is the snail? What do you think snails eat?
5. Why do you think the smaller fish are clustered around the roots of the tree?

Wrap up the discussion by explaining that animals use mangrove trees as a place to nest, find food, raise their young, and as protection from other animals that want to eat them. Then pass out markers or crayons and have the kids color their mangrove swamp scenes.

A MANGROVE SING-ALONG

After talking about mangrove swamps, try some singing and movement to help your kids remember what they've learned. Have the kids form a circle. As you lead the song below (to the tune of "Old MacDonald"), have the kids make the movements that go along with each animal. The suggested movements appear at the end of the song.

Pelicans live in mangrove trees,
e-i-e-i-o.
They build their nests among the leaves,
e-i-e-i-o.
With a *flap-flap* here and a *flap-flap* there,
Here a *flap*, there a *flap*, everywhere a *flap-flap*.
Pelicans live in mangrove trees,
e-i-e-i-o.

Rat snakes prowl the branches high,
e-i-e-i-o.
They gulp down eggs and birds they spy,
e-i-e-i-o.
With a *gulp-gulp* here and a *gulp-gulp* there, etc.

Crabs crawl in the mangrove trees,
e-i-e-i-o.
They snip off lots of mangrove leaves,
e-i-e-i-o.
With a *pinch-pinch* here, and a *pinch-pinch* there, etc.

Crocs live in the mangrove swamp,
e-i-e-i-o.
They catch their prey with a mighty chomp,
e-i-e-i-o.
With a *chomp-chomp* here and a *chomp-chomp* there, etc.

Oysters cling to the roots below,
e-i-e-i-o.
They filter out their food, you know,
e-i-e-i-o.
With a *slurp-slurp* here and a *slurp-slurp* there, etc.

Movements:
Pelican—flap arms up and down
Rat Snake—hold arms at sides and wiggle body
Crab—move thumbs back and forth like a pincer
Crocodile—have the left hand grab the right shoulder and the right hand grab the left shoulder and move elbows up and down in opposite directions
Oyster—keep heels of hands together as rest of hand opens and shuts

WHO'S WHO IN THE MANGROVE

WHITE IBIS
- nests in mangrove trees
- builds platform nest of twigs
- nests in colonies
- feeds on crabs and other small animals it picks out of mud at low tide

BROWN PELICAN
- makes sturdy nest of sticks, reeds, and twigs woven into the upper branches of mangrove trees
- usually nests in large colonies
- makes flying dives into the water to scoop up fish
- endangered in parts of the United States, but is now making a "comeback"

MANGROVE SNAPPER
- swims among submerged mangrove roots
- feeds on shrimp, small

crabs, and other crustaceans
- young stay among roots to hide from predators

BLUE CRAB
- has paddlelike fifth pair of legs that help it swim
- clings to roots when in "soft shell" stage after molting
- eats plant material, shrimp, small fish, oysters, clams, and animals that have recently died

AMERICAN CROCODILE
- waits among submerged mangrove roots for fish, mammals, and birds—quickly snaps up prey
- female builds nest of sticks and leaves
- is endangered; only a few hundred remain in the United States

YELLOW RAT SNAKE
- climbs among the trees
- is not poisonous
- eats rodents, birds, and eggs

SEA HORSE
- is a type of fish
- uses prehensile (grasping) tail to cling to mangrove roots
- father carries young in a brood pouch until they hatch
- eats plankton that it sucks in through tubelike mouth

OYSTER
- feeds on organic material by sucking in water through siphon and filtering out food
- attaches to prop roots with fingerlike extensions along shell
- grows in large clusters

GREEN-BACKED HERON
- builds platform nest of sticks in mangrove roots, only inches above high tide mark
- hunts for fish, frogs, insects, and small snakes in shallow water

MANGROVE TREE CRAB
- feeds on mangrove leaves
- lives in upper branches of mangrove trees
- if alarmed, drops from branches into the water

ANGULATE PERIWINKLE
- is one of the most abundant snails in mangrove swamps
- browses on algae and other plant material
- is found on roots and branches above high tide mark

Salty Discoveries

Hatch brine shrimp eggs and observe their development.

Objectives:
Design an experiment. Discuss the adaptability of saltwater wetland creatures.

Ages:
Primary, Intermediate, and Advanced

Materials:
- *white paper*
- *magnifying glasses*
- *brine shrimp eggs*
- *small, clear containers*
- *marine salt or non-iodized salt*
- *medicine droppers (optional)*
- *aged tapwater or spring water*
- *crayons or markers*
- *packaged yeast (optional)*

(continued next page)

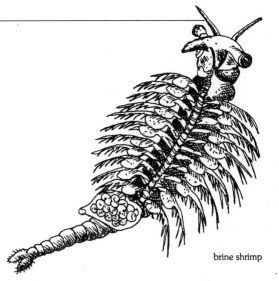

brine shrimp

Can you imagine spending your life swimming in salt water? Lots of creatures do, including those that live in salt marshes, mangrove swamps, and tidal flats. These animals all have built-in adaptations to deal with salt water. And many can live in fluctuating levels of salinity. By raising their own brine shrimp in water of different salinities, the kids in your group can see firsthand that many coastal wetland creatures are well adapted to changeable saltwater habitats. (*Note:* Brine shrimp live in saltwater lakes and in coastal salt pans. They usually are not found in coastal saltwater wetlands. However, they have some of the same adaptations to salt water as grass shrimp and other animals that *do* live in coastal wetlands. And they are easy to raise in a classroom or nature center.)

Start off by discussing the characteristics of saltwater wetlands, using the background information on pages 18-20. Then briefly tell the kids how some animals and plants in a salt marsh deal with the changing conditions. (See "Changing with the Tide" on page 27.)

Now pass out a sheet of white paper and a magnifying glass to each child. Sprinkle a few brine shrimp eggs onto each sheet, but don't tell the kids what they are. Ask the kids to describe them. What do they think they are?

Tell the kids that they're looking at the eggs of an animal that lives in saltwater lakes and, like the animals that live in saltwater wetlands, is adapted to salty conditions. Explain that the eggs hatch in salt water but that the kids must figure out just how salty the water should be.

Ask the kids how they could find out what amount of saltiness is best. Help them design an experiment to test their ideas. For example, they could set up several containers of water, put fresh water in one, and then put water that's increasingly salty in the others. You can mix up a few batches of salty water for the kids to use or let them make their own. Just be sure to use only spring water or aged tapwater in the mixtures, and have the kids label their containers. (One tablespoon [15 ml] of salt mixed with one cup [240 ml] of water is usually a good mixture for the eggs, so you might want to make your samples more or less salty around this ratio. Or you can let the kids discover a ratio for themselves.) Then have the kids add some eggs to each container and watch to see what happens. (It will take a day or two for the eggs to hatch.)

Once the shrimp have hatched, the kids can continue to observe them. Have them keep records on how long they live, how they move, what they look like, and so on. Younger kids can keep their records by drawing pictures. (Enough tiny algae and bacteria may grow in the containers to feed the brine shrimp. You may also want to add *small* amounts of

packaged yeast as well. [A pinch of yeast is all you need. Too much yeast can kill the shrimp.])

Older kids may want to design other brine shrimp experiments. For example, they might want to see what happens if they transfer the hatched shrimp to water of different salinities. Do the shrimp survive? How big a salinity change can they stand? The kids could also try to figure out if different temperatures affect the hatching of brine shrimp eggs. (For more about brine shrimp and brine shrimp experiments, see the *Teacher's Guide for Brine Shrimp* available from Delta Education [see below]).

After the kids have finished their experiments, have them report their results to the rest of the group. Then discuss what they found out. Brine shrimp, like many creatures that live in salt water, can tolerate very different salinities. These animals can remain relatively active even if the salinity isn't at an "optimum." Explain that many other creatures, such as mussels that live in salt water, are active in a narrower range of salinities. These creatures tend to shut down when conditions aren't "just perfect." (The salinity in a coastal wetland often changes drastically as the tides come and go and when it rains. Animals and plants that live in these areas must be able to cope with these conditions.)

Ellen Lambeth

SOLUTIONS TO SALT

Here's a brief look at a few of the adaptations that help coastal wetland creatures cope with salt.

- The shells of many saltwater creatures, such as crabs and some shrimp, are impervious to salt. The only way these animals can take up salt is through their food and water.
- Some animals, such as some crabs, bivalves, and seabirds, have special glands that excrete extra salt.
- Some animals, such as some fish, clams, and shrimp, can excrete salt across their gills.
- Some fish conserve water by excreting very concentrated urine.

Where to Get Brine Shrimp

Brine shrimp eggs and marine salt are available at most pet stores that carry aquarium supplies. Brine shrimp eggs, clear plastic containers, magnifying glasses, medicine droppers, marine salt, and a teacher's guide are also available in a kit called *Brine Shrimp* from Delta Education. (The teacher's guide and all of the other materials can be ordered separately too.) To order write Delta Education, P.O. Box M, Nashua, NH 03061-6012 or call (800) 258-1302. In NH, HI, and AK call (603) 889-8899 collect.

Note: This activity is adapted with permission from Delta Education Corporation.

Build a Mangrove

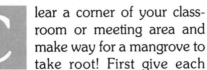

Clear a corner of your classroom or meeting area and make way for a mangrove to take root! First give each child a copy of page 31. Explain that this mangrove swamp scene shows some of the animals that live in mangrove trees. You can use the background information on page 23 to talk about these animals.

Then tell the kids that they'll be working together in groups to make a red mangrove tree complete with roots, branches, leaves, and wildlife. Divide the kids into three teams—the Trunk Team, the Root Team, and the Canopy Team. Directions on how to make the three parts of the tree are listed below. We've also included a short section on page 26 about how to make some of the animals that live on and around mangrove trees. (Have the kids look at their mangrove scenes to decide where the animals should go. Also see "Trees that Walk," *Ranger Rick,* Nov. 1986, pp 38-46, for more about mangrove swamps.) Then bring out construction paper, glue, scissors, tissue paper, egg cartons, and pipe cleaners, and watch that mangrove grow!

TRUNK

1. Tape or staple several sheets of brown or black construction paper together to form a trunk about one foot (30 cm) wide and three feet (90 cm) long.
2. Tape the trunk in the corner, attaching the sides of the trunk to the two walls. (This will give the effect of a three-dimensional tree.) The base of the trunk should be about two feet (60 cm) above the floor (see diagram on next page).
3. Create water around the mangrove by taping several sheets of blue tissue paper to the wall. The "sea" should reach from the floor to the base of the trunk.

ROOTS

1. Cut black or brown construction paper into long strips about 1 inch (2.5 cm) wide and 2-3 feet (60-90 cm) long. Also cut some shorter strips to make "accessory" roots that branch off the longer ones.
2. Beginning at the bottom of the trunk, tape the strips end to end to form roots reaching along both walls and extending away from the corner into the "water" (see diagram on next page). Anchor the roots by taping them to the floor.
3. Tape more strips along the main roots to make a maze of roots. Keep attaching more strips until the tangle of roots reaches into the water and a bit higher than the base of the trunk.

BRANCHES AND LEAVES (CANOPY)

1. Cut branches out of black or brown construction paper and tape them to the top of the trunk.
2. Use sheets of green tissue paper to make layers of leaves. Tape a few sheets of tissue paper together and attach to the two walls of the corner.
3. Add a few more layers of tissue paper, each one a little higher and a bit farther from the corner (see diagram on next page).
4. If you want to get more kids involved, have them cut out individual leaves from green construction paper and tape them to the branches.

(continued next page)

- For larger animals such as herons, pelicans, and crocodiles, cut outlines out of thin cardboard. Color them with crayons or markers and tape them in the appropriate places on the tree.
- Cut smaller animals (snakes, turtles, fish, and so on) out of construction paper and tape them on the tree.
- By following the directions at the right, you can also make crabs and snails out of egg cartons.

canopy tissue paper

tape to walls

trunk

roots

water

tape to floor

CRAB

1. Cut out one cup from the egg carton and turn it upside down.
2. On each side of the cup, poke four holes in a line about a half-inch (1.3 cm) above the bottom edge (see diagram). Also poke two holes in the front section of the cup.
3. Poke one pipe cleaner through a side hole and out the hole on the other side. Then bend the pipe cleaner ends downward to form the legs of the crab. Repeat with three other pipe cleaners.
4. Push a fifth pipe cleaner through the holes on the front of the crab, and bend the ends forward. These will form the clawed legs.
5. Cut claws and stalked eyes out of construction paper. Glue the eyes on the top of the cup and the claws on the ends of the pipe cleaner (see diagram).

SNAIL

1. Cut out one cup from an egg carton and turn it upside down.
2. Cut out a foot, head, and tentacles from construction paper and glue them to the cup (see diagram).

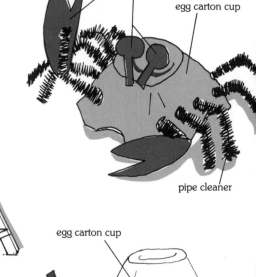

construction paper

egg carton cup

pipe cleaner

egg carton cup

construction paper

Changing with the Tide

Make a salt marsh display board to show how some animals are affected by the changing tides.

Objective:
Give several examples of how animals and plants are adapted to the changing conditions in a salt marsh.

Ages:
Intermediate and Advanced

Materials:
- *copies of page 32*
- *pieces of corrugated cardboard*
- *scissors*
- *glue*
- *crayons or markers*
- *construction paper*
- *thin cardboard*
- *paper*
- *yarn*
- *paper punch*
- *pictures of a salt marsh*
- *reference books*
- *chalkboard or easel paper*

Subject:
Science

In this activity the kids in your group will learn about some of the plants and animals that live in salt marshes and how their lives are influenced by the tides. (*Note:* The specific plants and animals in salt marshes in different parts of the country vary. Those discussed in this activity would be found in a salt marsh along the mid-Atlantic coast of the United States, though many are also found in salt marshes in other parts of the country.)

Before you get started, make a salt marsh board by following the directions on page 28. Then make some wearable salt marsh signs by writing "fiddler crab," "ribbed mussel," "raccoon," and "killifish" on separate sheets of paper, punching two holes in the paper, and threading a piece of yarn through the holes. Also make three or four signs for each of these plants: cordgrass, marsh hay, and spike grass. (You'll be using the board and the signs later on.) Then copy the picture at the top of the next page onto a chalkboard or large sheet of easel paper.

Begin by using the background information on pages 18-20 to explain the general characteristics of a salt marsh. Next tell the kids that the plants and animals in a salt marsh live in different parts of the marsh depending on how tolerant they are of salt, changes in salt concentrations, changes in temperature, and changes in water levels. For example, plants and animals that can withstand being alternately flooded for long periods of time and then left "high and dry" each day live in the part of the marsh that's closest to the sea. This area is called the *low* marsh. Plants and animals less tolerant of salt water live farther away from the sea in the *high* marsh. The high marsh is flooded for only a few hours each day or even just a few hours twice a month.

To get the kids thinking about what life in the marsh is like, try the following demonstration.

PART 1: LOW TIDE/HIGH TIDE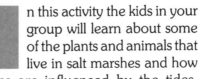

Have several kids volunteer to be salt marsh cordgrass and have them wear the cordgrass signs you made earlier. Have these kids stand near one side of a large, open area outside to represent the low marsh. Explain that in many salt marshes cordgrass is about the only plant that grows in the low marsh. Next, have a few kids volunteer to be some of the plants that grow in the high marsh—marsh hay and spike grass, for example. Give these kids the appropriate signs to wear and have them stand next to the cordgrass. Then have a few kids wear the salt marsh animal signs and stand aside. (They'll be in the salt marsh later.) Finally, have the rest of the kids become the salt water.

Start off by having the water be at low tide. (The "ocean" should be at the far end of the cordgrass, on the side farthest away from the plants of the high marsh.) Then make the water rise by having the ocean slowly walk up through the low marsh plants and into the high marsh plants. Then have the tide flow out again.

After the tide has risen and fallen once or twice, ask the kids which plants were covered by water for the longest time. (cordgrass) Then have the animals come into the salt marsh. First have the ribbed mussel and fiddler crab stand in the low marsh and explain that these animals both live in the low marsh. What do the kids think these animals might do as the tide comes and goes? (See "Plants and Animals of the Salt Marsh" on page 29.) Next have the raccoon stand in the high marsh and the killifish stand in the ocean and ask the kids what they think these animals might do as the tide comes and goes. (Depending on the size of your group, you may want to include other animals.)

Once again, have the tide rise and fall. But as the tide moves in and out, have the animals act out what they would do in a real salt marsh. (For example, to hide in its burrow the fiddler crab could crouch down low. And the killifish could swim into the marsh with the tide.)

(continued next page)

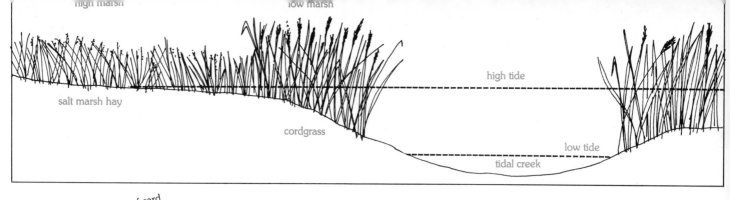

high marsh   low marsh

high tide

salt marsh hay

cordgrass

low tide

tidal creek

line up top of picture with top of card

tab   cut

cut

scratch slit in board

PART 2: DISPLAY BOARDS

Now pass out copies of page 32. Explain that the pictures on the top half of the page show what some salt marsh animals might be doing when the tide is out. The pictures on the bottom half of the page show what some of these animals, plus a few others, might be doing while the tide is in. Using the information on the next page and the display board that you made earlier, talk about each of the creatures on the sheet as well as some of the plants that live in salt marshes.

Afterward, pass out thin cardboard, scissors, glue, crayons or markers, construction paper, and pieces of corrugated cardboard (the sides of boxes work well) and have the kids follow these directions to make their own salt marsh boards:

1. Color the pictures on page 32 and cut them out. (Be sure the kids keep the low tide and high tide pictures in separate piles. You may want to have the kids label each picture "LT" or "HT" to help keep them straight.)

2. Cut out six rectangles from the thin cardboard (about 2½ × 3½″ [6.3 × 8.8 cm]).

3. Glue each of the low tide pictures to a separate card and let dry. (Line up the top edge of each picture with the top edge of the card so that you have excess cardboard along the bottom edge for a tab [see step 4].) Then glue a high tide picture to the back of each card.

4. Trim the bottom edge of each card to form a tab (see diagram).

5. Use pointed scissors to make six slits in the display board. The slits should be just a little longer than the tabs on the cards and should be spread out on the board. Use a pencil to mark how long each slit should be. Then hold the scissors completely open and *scratch* a slit between the marks. (Don't press too hard or you'll crush the board.)

6. Make one end of the board the high marsh and the other end the low marsh. Use construction paper to decorate it. For example, you can fringe dark green construction paper for cordgrass and fringe light green paper to make marsh hay. You can also make other salt marsh plants, a tidal creek, or any other decorations. (Pass out reference books and encourage the kids to decorate their boards accurately.) Glue the decorations onto the board between the slits.

7. Place a card in each slit so that all of the low tide pictures face the same direction. Then, to show what happens when the tide comes in, remove each card, turn it around, and put it back in.

Adapted from *Smithsonian Estuarine Activities* with permission from the Smithsonian Institution.

Note: Some of these animals and plants are found on both the Atlantic and Pacific coasts. For those found only on the Atlantic coast, we've listed similar Pacific coast species in parentheses at the end of each section.

Blue Crab—Moves into marsh as tide rises. Feeds on worms, snails, oysters, and other marine animals. Moves out of the marsh with the tide. Breathes with gills. If gets caught in salt marsh as tide goes out, it will bury itself in the mud and wait for the tide to rise again. (yellow shore crab)

Clam Worm—Burrows in mud of salt marsh and as it burrows it secretes slime that "glues" sand grains together and then hardens into a flexible tube. When tide covers the mud it may come out of its tube and swim around looking for food. Feeds on other worms, dead fish, other soft-bodied animals, and algae. Remains in tube while tide is out. Is very tolerant of changes in salinity.

Clapper Rail—Nests in drier areas of high marsh. Feeds mostly at low tide along mud flats and along creek banks in the salt marsh. Eats fiddler crabs, worms, snails, small fish, and other marine animals. Hides in grass of high marsh during high tide.

Fiddler Crab—Digs burrows in mud or sand of the low marsh. Feeds on algae, bacteria, and decaying plant and animal matter that covers the surface of the mud. Comes out of its burrow at low tide to feed. Breathes air with gills that must be kept moist. Returns to burrow and may plug it with sand or mud during high tide. Can withstand long periods without oxygen. Can live in varying concentrations of salt water. (California fiddler crab)

Great Blue Heron—Hunts in shallow water of the salt marsh. Grabs fish with its long, sharp bill. May also eat shrimp, insects, small

mammals, and other animals in the marsh. As tide rises, moves higher on the marsh (to stay in shallow water) or may leave the marsh completely.

Killifish—Lives in shallow waters of the salt marsh. Moves into and out of the higher parts of the marsh with the tides. Feeds on mosquito larvae and other small animals as well as plants. Can withstand low concentrations of oxygen. (California killifish)

Raccoon—Comes to the salt marsh to hunt. Feeds on crabs, clams, fish, and other animals. Leaves the low marsh as the tide rises.

Ribbed Mussel—Lives half-buried in the mud of the low marsh where the tide floods regularly. Feeds on tiny plants and animals suspended in the water. Breathes with gills. While submerged, pumps water through its body, across its gills, and out again. Filters out food as the water passes through. When uncovered by water, leaves its shells slightly open so it can continue to breathe. If conditions get too bad, closes its shells completely and "holds its breath" until the tide returns.

Salt Marsh Snail—Usually lives in high marsh. Feeds on algae and bits of decaying grass on the surface of the mud. Lacks an operculum (see page 21), so during the day it crawls under the mat of dead marsh hay at low tide to keep from drying out. Breathes air with a lung. Crawls up spartina stalks (see below) during high tide to escape the water. Can "hold its breath" for one to two hours if it becomes submerged. (California salt marsh snail)

Spartina—Absorbs water through its roots without absorbing much salt. Salt that is absorbed is secreted through its leaves. Its long leaves also get rid of excess heat. Mud in salt marsh has very little oxygen in it but air tubes connect the surface of the spartina leaves with the roots and bring air down to them. Two major species grow in many salt marshes. Cordgrass grows in the low marsh where it gets flooded by water for long periods of time each day and can even be completely submerged by the highest high tides. Marsh hay grows in the high marsh where it gets flooded for only a few hours each day or even just a few hours each month.

Other Plants—Spike grass, blackgrass, salt marsh aster, sea lavender, seaside plantain, and many other plants may grow among the marsh hay and in the highest parts of the salt marsh. Some, such as spike grass, have a high saltwater tolerance and can stand being flooded by the tide periodically. But others, such as sea lavender, can withstand only occasional salt spray. (The plants in western salt marshes are often different from those in eastern salt marshes. Several kinds of spartina grasses grow in western marshes, but other plants are often more abundant. Depending on where a marsh is located along the Pacific Coast, there may be pickleweed, spike grass, sedges, salt rush, tule, milkwort, Pacific silverweed, and/or other plants.)

fiddler crab

MAKE A MUD SNAIL

siphon

eye

tentacle

proboscis

foot

shell

operculum

CHANGING WITH THE TIDE

LOW TIDE

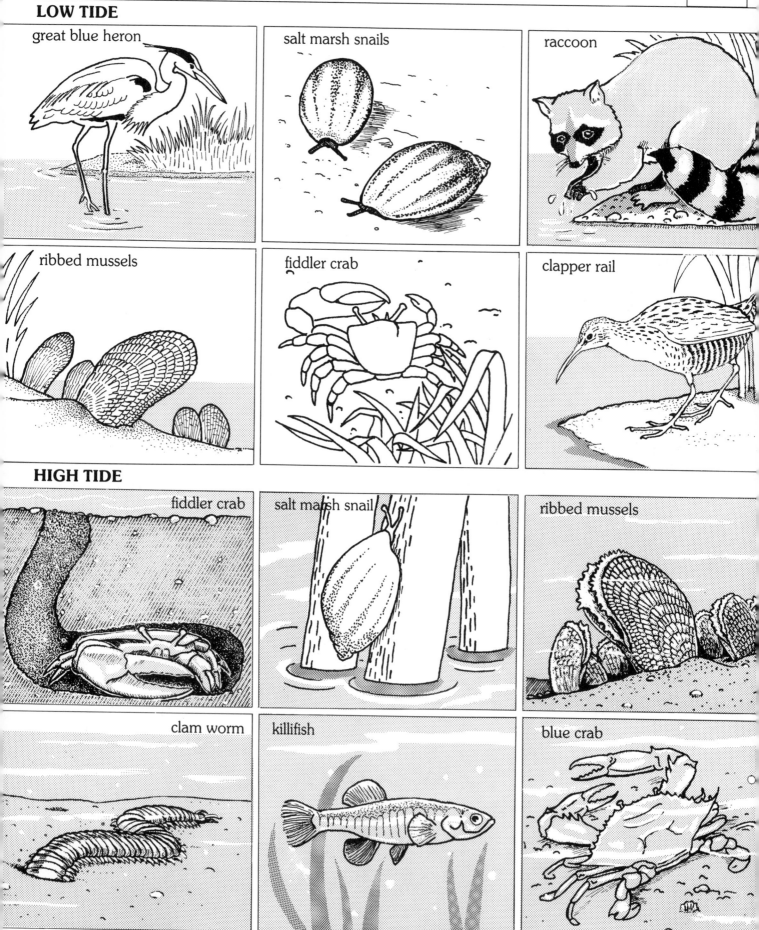

great blue heron

salt marsh snails

raccoon

ribbed mussels

fiddler crab

clapper rail

HIGH TIDE

fiddler crab

salt marsh snail

ribbed mussels

clam worm

killifish

blue crab

FRESHWATER WETLANDS

There's a duck factory in the Midwest. No, it's not a huge assembly line that pumps out plastic ducklings. It's a marshy wetland area, better known as prairie pothole country, that covers more than 300,000 square miles (780,000 km^2) throughout parts of the Dakotas, Minnesota, Montana, Iowa, and Canada. Millions of ducks—from mallards to ruddy ducks—start their lives here, as do thousands of geese, shorebirds, and other types of wildlife. Because of its incredible productivity, many scientists consider this prairie pothole region to be one of the most important wetland areas in the world.

In this chapter we'll focus on prairie potholes and other types of freshwater marshes. We'll also take a look at swamps and bogs and at the characteristics that make all freshwater wetlands unique.

Some scientists estimate that more than 50 percent of the wild ducks in North America depend on the prairie pothole region.

MARSHES

Millions of Marshes: From small cattail marshes along major highways in California to huge expanses of sawgrass in Florida, freshwater marshes are a common sight throughout much of North America. According to some biologists, freshwater marshes make up about 90 percent of our wetlands.

As in other types of wetlands, the water in a marsh often fluctuates from season to season, rising during heavy rainfalls and often disappearing during dry periods. But you can usually tell a marsh from other types of freshwater wetlands by the type of vegetation that grows there. Thick clumps of soft-stemmed plants such as grasses, sedges, and rushes are abundant. And cattails, water lilies, smartweeds, arrowheads, and other non-woody marsh plants are also common.

Types of Marshes: It's hard to generalize about freshwater marshes, but some scientists have lumped them into three general groups or zones:

- DEEP MARSHES are usually flooded every year, except during extreme droughts. The water can be up to four feet (1.2 m) deep during wet periods, and there are often areas of open water. Deep marshes are usually found near the edges of lakes, ponds, and rivers, but also form in deeper potholes. Most are fed by rainfall, storm runoff, and melting snow. Cattails, bulrushes, water lilies, and duckweed are common deep marsh plants.
- SHALLOW MARSHES are often found next to deep marshes. They are less regularly and less deeply flooded than deep marshes, and the water level is usually only six inches (15 cm) to a foot (30 cm) deep. Grasses and sedges are common shallow marsh plants, as are smartweeds, cattails, and bur reeds.
- WET MEADOWS flood annually and their soils may be saturated with water year round, but the water never gets deep. Many water-loving marsh plants, such as sedges, grasses, rushes, and wetland wildflowers, are common. Wet meadows form in poorly drained, low-lying areas and along streams or lakes.
Note: Many marshy areas, such as the prairie pothole region mentioned in the introduction, have a combination of these three types of marshes.

(continued next page)

Life Support Systems: "Teeming with wildlife" is an accurate description of many freshwater marshes. In fact, many scientists think that some marshes are the most productive habitats on Earth. Marshes provide food, shelter, and water for many animals, and they act as nurseries for young fish, birds, insects, mammals, reptiles, and other animals.

BOGS

For Peat's Sake: Peat, acid, and water. These three words characterize many of the world's bogs. Bogs are freshwater wetlands that usually contain a huge build-up of *peat*—rich organic material that is made up mostly of partially decayed plant material. Peat forms as plants die and their leaves, stems, roots, and other parts fall into the water. Over time, this acid-rich material is compressed, forming thick layers of peat. In some bogs, the peat can be over 40 feet (12 m) thick.

Bogs are usually found in the colder regions of the world. They form in wet areas where there is very little water flowing in or out of the wetland. The rate of decomposition in a bog is extremely slow, so the peat layer grows year after year. (The high acidity of the peat, the cold year-round temperatures, and the limited oxygen supply due to poor water circulation discourage bacteria and other decomposers from breaking down plant material.)

Buried Bog Treasures: Because of this slow rate of decomposition, plants and animals that fall into bogs often stay well-preserved for thousands of years. Scientists have dug into bog bottoms to find ancient pollen, leaves, and other plant parts, as well as perfectly preserved animal parts from prehistoric times. They've even found complete human bodies, with hair, muscles, and teeth intact.

Scientists have also been able to find and analyze buried sediments, such as radioactive fallout and heavy metals. By studying layered bog remains, they have pieced together information about how climates, vegetation, and landscapes have changed over time.

Quakin' and Shakin': The water in many bogs is covered with a floating mat of thick vegetation. In some bogs, the mat starts forming when sphagnum moss invades the tangled mass of aquatic plants that have grown in the open water. Eventually the sphagnum grows into a mossy mat and sometimes the entire bog becomes carpeted. The sphagnum also acts as a substrate for other plants. In time, even trees, such as black spruce and tamarack, will grow on the thick mat. If you walk on this mossy carpet, you can often feel it quiver and bounce with each step. The interconnected mat of sphagnum, plant roots, and peat underneath gives the bog its bounce because the entire vegetative mass floats in the water like a huge sponge.

An Icy Past: Many bogs in North America can thank glaciers for their start. About 10,000 years ago, when the last of the glaciers retreated, they left many glacial lakes behind. In some areas these lakes, called *kettle holes,* formed when huge blocks of glacial ice that had been buried underground melted. Others formed when shallow basins left by the retreating ice filled with rainwater. (Some bogs also form in unglaciated, poorly drained lakebeds and depressions.)

Life in the Bog: Many of the plants that live in bogs are specially adapted to high acidity, low oxygen and nutrient supplies, and a soggy substrate. Some bog plants, such as black spruce, have special root systems that are well adapted to dealing with low oxygen supplies and waterlogged conditions. Others, such as some orchids and heath plants, have symbiotic relationships with fungi, which helps them get the nutrients they need. And many bog plants, such as bladderworts, pitcher plants, and sundews, get some of their food in a very unusual way—they trap and digest insects and other tiny animals.

Bogs also support a wide variety of wildlife, although many animals are not full-time bog residents. For example, moose, deer, bears, and other large mammals visit bogs at various times of the year to find food, shelter, and water.

coons in den tree   Irene Vandermolen

Don't Get "Bogged Down": The word *bog* means different things to different people. In some parts of the world, it is used only when referring to acidic, sphagnum wetlands. In other places it is used to describe any type of wetland that has peat deposits. (Many scientists use the more general word *peatland* to describe a wetland that has peat deposits. And they consider bogs to be one type of peatland. Fens, carrs, and even some swamps and salt marshes are also considered to be types of peatlands because they contain peat deposits.) In this issue we are generally referring to acidic, sphagnum bogs when we say the word "bog."

SWAMPS

Swamp Stories: *Poisonous snakes hang from the trees. Quicksand is around every bend. Once you get lost, you'll never find your way out.* Considering the abundance of these and other myths, it's no wonder that many people have strange ideas about swamps. But most spooky swamp images have been the product of imaginative writers, and have little to do with reality. Yes, there are poisonous snakes in some swamps, but most don't climb or hang from trees. Quicksand occurs in some swampy areas, but it's not very common. And you are just as likely to get lost in a desert, forest, or other habitat as you are in a swamp.

The truth is that swamps are some of the most fascinating and diverse wetlands in the world. And they are no more dangerous than other types of habitats. From the cypress swamps of the Big Thicket in Texas to New Jersey's Great Swamp, each has its own character and unique plant and animal life.

Down in the Swamp: So what makes a swamp a swamp? Scientists define swamps as wetlands that are dominated by shrubs or trees. They are usually saturated with water during the growing season, but may dry out in late summer. Swamps can have anywhere from a few inches to a foot or more of water. In northern swamps red maple, black willow, northern white cedar, alder, and cottonwood are some of the more common trees. In southern swamps the forests are made up of such trees as water oak, tupelo, and bald cypress. And in some swamp areas, where shrubs are the most dominant plants, you'll find water willow, pussy willow, leatherleaf, inkberry, and buttonbush growing in the mucky soil.

Types of Swamps: There are many different types of freshwater swamps, but most fall into these two general groups:

- FORESTED SWAMPS are often associated with major river systems, such as the Mississippi, and they often occur on river floodplains. Many of these swamps are famous for their huge trees, and contain stands of enormous bald cypress, overcup oak, and tupelo. Most forested swamps are subjected to periodic flooding and usually stay wet during most of the year.
- SHRUB SWAMPS in North America are characterized by scrubby, low-growing vegetation. Some of these shallow swamps are wet for only part of the year and often dry out during hot, dry summers. There are many different types of shrub swamps, from boggy, boreal swamps in the north called *heaths* to shrubby coastal swamps in the southeast called *pocosins.* Shrub swamps often form in poorly drained areas on the edges of lakes, forested swamps, marshes, and streams.

Zoo in the Goo: Swamps are incredibly diverse and support a wide variety of animal life. Many swamp critters, such as alligators and cottonmouths, are especially adapted to the murky environment of a swamp. But others that usually live in upland areas, such as panthers, foxes, bears, and raccoons, often wander into swamps to find food, shelter, and water. (See "Gator Hole Graphics" on page 40 for more about life in a swamp.)

Little Green Monsters

Distinguish real wetland plants from imaginary ones.

Objective:
Name several freshwater wetland plants and describe how they are adapted to their habitats.

Ages:
Primary and Intermediate

Materials:
- *copies of page 42*
- *pictures of wetland plants (see activity for suggestions)*
- *construction paper*
- *scissors*
- *glue*
- *crayons or markers*
- *stapler*
- *pencils*

Subject:
Science

round-leaved sundew

Some of these plants devour insects, others can soak up to 25 times their weight in water, and one can produce enough heat to melt snow. It may sound like science fiction, but certain wetland plants can really do these things. In this activity your kids will be separating imaginary wetland "monsters" from real plants that are just as weird.

Pass out a pencil and a copy of page 42 to each child. Tell the kids that some of the plants on the page are real wetland plants. (Point out that our cartoons don't look exactly like the real plants. For example, real plants don't have eyes!) As you briefly discuss each plant (using the numbered information below), the kids must decide if the plant is real or not. If they think the plant really does exist, they should circle the number next to the plant.

The background information we've provided includes brief descriptions of each plant. For the quiz, read only the information that is in color. (Don't read the names of the plants.) You can add the additional information later when you discuss the plants that are real. Tell the kids to concentrate on the explanations you read to decide if the plants are real or not.

After the kids have finished, discuss their answers and tell them which plants are real. Also show them pictures of the real "monsters" as you discuss them.

BACKGROUND INFORMATION

1. **(Venus Flytrap—real):** This plant has sensitive trigger hairs on the inside of each leaf. If an insect brushes against at least two hairs, the leaf will close up, trapping the insect. Then the plant gradually digests the insect's soft parts, leaving the hard parts "uneaten."

   This carnivorous plant grows in the marshes of North and South Carolina. Today, Venus flytraps are rare because many people have dug up the plants to take home or sell in plant shops.
   Note: In the discussion you may want to point out to the kids that, like all other *carnivorous* plants, Venus flytraps *can* grow without digesting insects or other small creatures. (Like other plants, carnivorous plants make food through photosynthesis.) But they will grow better with an "animal supplement" to their diets. Insects and other small creatures provide nutrients that aren't abundant in some wetlands.

2. **(Three-Leaved Stick 'Um Plant— imaginary):** This small plant has a special way of getting around. Its seeds stick onto the fur of passing animals. The plant sprouts while still on an animal and grows there for a few weeks. During this time it survives on food stored in its seed coat. When it reaches a certain size, it drops off and takes root.

3. **(Hooded Pitcher Plant—real):** Each of this plant's leaves forms a special "pitcher," and nectar on the lip of the pitcher attracts insects. But the surface around the lip is very slippery. As the insects crawl or land near the lip, many fall into the long, hollow leaf that ends in a pool of water and digestive acids.

   Downward-pointing hairs and the slippery walls of the plant prevent insects from crawling up and out of the "pitcher." The insects drown and are slowly digested until nothing remains but their hard outer coverings and wings.

   Hooded pitcher plants have another trick that is unique among the different kinds of pitcher plants. They have transparent "windows" in the back of their "hoods" that look like escape routes. Insects that attempt to fly away crash into the hood, then fall into the pool below.

   These plants grow in marshes, bogs, and other wetlands from North Carolina to Florida.

Venus flytrap

4. (Shoveler Plant—imaginary): This wetland plant has a special adaptation that helps it survive in overcrowded areas. As it breaks through the soil, two large, thick leaves grow on either side of the main bud. These leaves grow outward and uproot any other plants that are in the way.

5. (Round-Leaved Sundew—real): The leaves of this plant are covered with many short stalks. Each stalk is tipped with sticky nectar. Insects attracted to the nectar land on the stalks and become stuck. As they struggle to escape, they come in contact with more stalks and become more firmly trapped. The stalks slowly move the insect to the center of the leaf. The edges of the leaf then slowly fold around the insect, and digestion begins.

The sundew gets its name from the way sunlight glistens on the liquid-tipped hairs.

6. (Horned Bladderwort—real): This water-dwelling plant eats small aquatic insects and other animals. Its leaves and stalks are lined with many small, balloonlike bladders. Each bladder has a trapdoor. If a small insect brushes against the sensitive hairs around the trapdoor, it is quickly sucked through the trapdoor and slowly digested.

Bladderworts grow in the shallow waters of marshes, bogs, and swamps.

7. (Sphagnum Moss—real): This plant often grows in open water or on the surface of moist soil. Gas-filled cells keep it floating near the water's surface. The cells are specially designed to soak up water. In fact, each plant can absorb as much as 25 times its own weight in water! The plant uses this extra water during droughts.

Sphagnum moss is often the first plant to grow in a bog. Younger plants grow on top of older plants. As the older layers die, they eventually form thick deposits of peat. In the past, people have used the peat to heat their homes, stop wounds from bleeding, and to make super-absorbent baby diapers. Today, people use it mostly to condition the soil in their gardens.

8. (Tentacle Plant—imaginary): This plant has long, sticky tentacles that grow out in all directions from its base. If an insect—or some other small creature—touches a tentacle, it gets stuck. The tentacle slowly curls around the victim, squeezing it tightly. Nutrients are sucked from the victim and passed through the tentacle to the rest of the plant.

9. (Skunk Cabbage—real): This plant begins growing very early in the spring each year—sometimes when snow is still on the ground. As the plant pushes through the soil, it produces heat by breaking down food reserves stored in its roots. The plant may get so warm that it melts the snow surrounding it! This heat helps protect its delicate flower.

Scientists aren't sure why the skunk cabbage starts growing so early each year. But they think it must give the plant some advantage over the other plants growing in the area. Skunk cabbage has another unusual adaptation. It gives off a skunklike odor that attracts flies and other insects, which help pollinate the plant.

horned bladderwort

water level

hooded pitcher plant

BRANCHING OUT: MONSTER BOOKLETS

To help them remember what they've learned about these real wetland plants, the kids can make their own "monster" booklets. Have them color and cut out the pictures of real plants. Then they can stack three sheets of construction paper together, fold them in half, and staple them.

Finally, have them glue each picture onto a separate page and write the names of the plants below the drawings.

As a follow-up, take your group on a trip to a botanical garden in your area. Many have carnivorous plants on display.

Hidden in the Marsh

Make a paper model of a freshwater marsh community.

Objectives:
Name several animals that live in freshwater marshes. Describe how marsh plants help these animals survive.

Ages:
Intermediate

Materials:
- copies of page 43
- construction paper
- field guides and other reference books
- scissors
- glue
- crayons or markers
- pens or sharpened pencils
- stapler or tape

Subjects:
Science and Art

In many freshwater marshes, cattails and certain other plants are the "pillars" of the community. They provide food and shelter for ducks, blackbirds, muskrats, and other marsh animals, and their leaves and other parts make great nesting material.

Have your kids make their own movable marsh scenes to learn more about some freshwater marsh plants and the animals that depend on them. Begin by discussing the general characteristics of a freshwater marsh. (See the background information on pages 33-34.) Then talk about the role that marsh plants play in the ecology of the marsh. For example, muskrats eat their roots, caterpillars and other insects munch on their leaves, blackbirds nest on their stalks, and ducks hide their nests among them. And as marsh plants die and decompose, they provide food for microscopic animals, which are in turn eaten by larger animals. They also return nutrients to the soil, helping other plants to grow.

After your discussion, let the kids get started on their scenes. Give each child a copy of page 43 and a piece of construction paper. Also provide glue, scissors, and crayons or markers. Then have the kids follow the directions we've provided at the end of the activity.

When the kids are finished making their marsh scenes, discuss each of the plants and animals using the information below. (You can identify all the animals and plants in both inserts by referring to the diagrams.) *Note:* You can have the kids color just one or both of the inserts—we've included two to increase the variety of animals you can talk about. (The plants are the same in both inserts.) The animals in insert A are common in freshwater marshes in the eastern United States, and those in insert B are animals you'd be likely to see in a midwestern prairie pothole. But many of the animals overlap. For example, you could find muskrats and minks in a prairie pothole as well as in an eastern marsh. And some kinds of butterflies and ducks live in both western and eastern marshes.

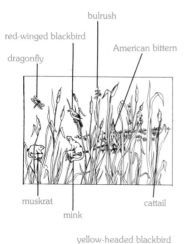

INSERT A

Cattails: These plants grow in both deep and shallow marshes. They store food in underground stems called rootstalks. Muskrats and other marsh animals eat these rootstalks. And many marsh birds eat cattail seeds and use the leaves to build their nests.

Bulrushes: Bulrushes grow along streams, ponds, marshes, and other wet areas. They have long, spearlike stems topped with small, hard flowers. Muskrats, ducks, and other marsh animals eat bulrush roots, and ducks often eat their seeds.

American bittern: Bitterns spend most of their time poking around for fish, frogs, and other animals among marsh plants. They also feed on small mammals and snakes that live in marshy areas. If danger is near, these herons point their long bills and necks upward. This helps them to blend in with the tall marsh plants. Bitterns also use cattails and other marsh plants to build their nests. The nests are placed on the ground or in shallow water, where they're well hidden among the thick vegetation.

Red-winged blackbird: These birds eat mostly insects. They often build their nests on old cattail stalks. Males often perch on the stalks to watch over their territories, and they spend a lot of time chasing other males away.

Muskrat: Muskrats are rodents that are adapted to an aquatic life. Their partially webbed hind feet help them swim, and their flattened tails act like rudders. Muskrats eat several kinds of marsh plants, but depend heavily on cattail roots. They also use shredded cattails and other marsh plants to build their lodges.

Mink: Minks don't rely directly on marsh plants for food or nesting material. But many of the animals they feed on depend on marsh vegetation. For example, minks prey heavily on muskrats.

Dragonfly: Cattails and bulrushes serve as "landing pads" for dragonflies. These insects sometimes perch on marsh plants when they're not patrolling their territories or hunting for mosquitoes and other prey.

Yellow-headed blackbird: These insect-eaters live in the western half of the United States. Yellow-headed blackbird males perch on cattail stalks or reeds as they defend their territories. In areas where they overlap, male yellow-headed and red-winged blackbirds often compete for territories—and yellow-headed blackbirds usually win.

Ruddy duck: Like many other types of waterfowl, these small ducks rely on prairie potholes for breeding. They also stop to rest and feed in potholes during migration. Ruddy ducks eat insects, snails, and some marsh plants. They build their nests with cattails, sedges, and grasses. The nests are usually hidden among marsh plants.

male ruddy duck

Len Rue, Jr.

leopard frog

Alvin E. Staffan

Whitetail deer: These big browsers are only visitors to marshes. Female deer often leave their fawns hidden in tall marsh grasses while they feed near the marsh.

Northern eyed brown: Growing caterpillars eat bulrushes and some other marsh plants. The adult butterflies sip nectar from plants growing around the marsh.

Northern leopard frog: Leopard frogs usually sit among marsh plants near areas of standing or open water. If a leopard frog senses danger, into the water it goes! Adult leopard frogs eat insects. And the tadpoles, which hatch and develop in the marsh waters, eat algae at first and then insect larvae and other tiny aquatic creatures.

HOW TO MAKE A MOVABLE MARSH

1. Color the plants on the frame and the animals and plants on inserts A and B. (Have the kids look in field guides and other reference books for pictures of the animals and plants so they can color them accurately.)
2. Glue the Copycat Page onto a piece of construction paper and let it dry. (Cover the entire back of the page with a *thin* layer of glue.)
3. Cut out the frame and the two inserts along the solid black lines.
4. Carefully cut out the windows on the frame along the dotted lines. (To help the kids start cutting, have them use a pencil or pen to poke a hole in a corner of each window.)

5. Fold the frame in half along the dotted "fold" line so that the construction paper is on the inside.
6. Hold the frame lengthwise so the folded edge is on the left. Staple or tape together the top and bottom edges of the frame.
7. Slide one of the inserts into the frame. (The illustrated side should be facing up, and the word "pull" should be on the right-hand side.) When the insert is all the way in, only the marsh plants will be visible. Have the kids slowly pull out the insert until all the animals are visible.
8. You may want to have the kids write the names of the plants and animals on the backs of their inserts to help them remember what they've learned.

pull

Gator Hole Graphics

Interpret graphs that
tell how some swamp
animals survive drought.

Objectives:
*Describe some of the
ways drought affects
animals in a swamp.
Explain why alligators
are an important part of
the swamp community.*

Ages:
Advanced

Materials:
- *copies of pages 44
  and 45*
- *map of the United
  States*
- *pencils*
- *chalkboard or easel
  paper*
- *rulers*
- *graph paper*

Subjects:
Science and Math

Swamp Food Web

ater is probably the first word that comes to mind when you think about wetlands. But in some swamps, water periodically becomes as hard to find as it is in some deserts. In this activity your kids can see how animals adapt to a seasonal lack of water in Florida's Big Cypress Swamp.

Tell the kids that they'll be learning about the Big Cypress Swamp. Begin by explaining that Big Cypress covers an area of about 2000 square miles (5200 km²) in southern Florida on the western edge of the Everglades. Have one of the kids point out the swamp on a map.

Next copy the simplified swamp food web shown below on a chalkboard or piece of easel paper. As the kids look at the drawing, ask them to name some of the predators in the swamp. (snakes, river otters, alligators) Then ask them to name some of the prey animals. (insects, mosquitofish, frogs) Can they explain what the arrows mean? (The arrows point from an animal to the animal that eats it.) Point out that some animals, such as frogs and snakes, can be both predators and prey.

Next tell the kids that in the late 1960s a scientist named Dr. Jim Kushlan decided to study how the changing seasons in Big Cypress affect the animals that live there. Listed below are the things he observed. (You may want to list the major points on a chalkboard or large piece of easel paper to help the kids follow along. Also copy the diagrams in the margin so the kids can get a better understanding of what's happening.)

- There is usually a six-month period each year when the average monthly rainfall is very low. During this dry season the shallow sheet of water that usually covers the swamp disappears, leaving only isolated ponds and a few large bodies of water.
- Many species of fish, birds, reptiles, and mammals rely on the larger and deeper bodies of water, such as lakes and canals, to survive the dry season.

- Ponds scattered throughout the swamp also attract large numbers of wildlife. These ponds are called alligator ponds, or "gator holes," because each is usually occupied by an adult female alligator. Many of these ponds are created whan an alligator digs a den in the swamp ground. And in times of severe drought, when even the water in the gator holes has dried up, alligators sometimes dig deeper into the ground to reach the water below the surface.
- Gator holes have few water plants growing in them. By dragging their heavy bodies through the ponds, gators enlarge the ponds and keep the water vegetation from growing.
- Gator holes are great habitats for fish. And the fish provide food for wading birds, reptiles, and mammals.

Point out to the kids that alligators don't purposefully create and maintain gator holes to keep other animals alive. But due to their normal habits, they create this open-water habitat that helps other kinds of animals survive the dry season.

When his study was completed, Dr. Kushlan wrote a paper explaining what he had learned. His paper included graphs that illustrated his data and a summary of what he concluded from his research.

Now pass out copies of page 44. Tell the kids the graphs on the page represent part of his data. Then pass out copies of page 45. Have the kids study the graphs, then answer the questions on page 45. After they've finished, discuss the answers listed on page 41.

Note: The graphs and data in this activity were adapted from the actual study conducted by Dr. James A. Kushlan in Big Cypress Swamp.

1. June; December; November through April

2. April. Tell the kids that at this point the land around the gator hole has dried up and it has become an isolated source of water. Refer them back to the two diagrams you copied earlier.

3. April

4. During the dry season, between the months of March and April. Point out that these additional species came from the surrounding swamp waters that dried up as the dry season continued. Explain that many fish and other animals died during the drought. But enough individuals managed to follow the receding waters into the gator hole.

5. a

6. False. The greatest number of alligators occupied the gator hole in April, when the water level was at its lowest mark—30 inches.

   Explain that the total number of alligators in the swamp doesn't change much from wet season to dry season, but the distribution of alligators throughout the swamp does. During the wet season, young alligators and adult males usually wander throughout the swamp. (Only adult females live in gator holes year round.) But as the swamp dries up, the "wanderers" head for remaining water. Resident females will sometimes tolerate young alligators at their ponds, although the females have been observed eating a few "visitors." Males and some of the youngsters gather at larger bodies of water, such as lakes and canals.

7. c

8. Increase. All these animals flock to gator holes to eat fish. This predation actually helps a greater number of fish survive. If none of the fish were eaten by predators, most would die from lack of oxygen. This way, some fish are eaten, but the remaining fish have enough oxygen to last until the rains return.

9. In years with heavy rainfall, isolated ponds crowded with fish do not form. Because of their unique fishing technique, wood storks have a harder time catching fish that are not packed together. Under these conditions, it would take more time and energy for parents fishing one at a time to catch enough fish to feed their young. Rather than attempting to raise young that may not survive, wood storks do not breed at all during very wet years.

10. The pond was filled by the heavy rains that fell from May through October. After several months of very little rain, the water in the pond had evaporated down to April's low level.

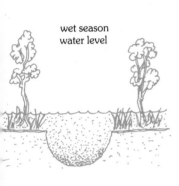

wet season water level

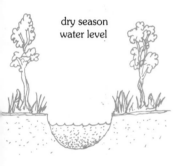

dry season water level

BRANCHING OUT: PROBLEMS ON THE PRAIRIE

To illustrate wetland loss, have your kids try this prairie pothole graphing activity. First discuss what prairie potholes are and where they're located, using the background information on pages 33-34. Then copy the table at the right on a chalkboard or piece of easel paper. Pass out graph paper, pencils, and rulers to the kids, and have them graph the data. (You can also have the kids convert acres to hectares and graph these numbers [conversion factor: acres × 0.4 = hectares].)

Afterward, ask the kids what happened between 1974 and 1983. How do they think this loss of habitat might affect wildlife that depends on prairie potholes? Explain that the numbers of ducks, geese, and other waterfowl in this area have decreased, and that most scientists agree that the loss of prairie pothole marshes is a major reason for this decline.

YEAR	NUMBER OF ACRES
1974	2,180,000
1975	2,160,000
1976	2,145,000
1977	2,120,000
1978	2,100,000
1979	2,085,000
1980	2,060,000
1981	2,035,000
1982	2,020,000
1983	2,000,000

Note: This data is based on an estimate of average yearly wetland losses in North Dakota. In this state alone about 20,000 acres (8000 ha) are drained and developed each year. Most of these former wetlands become cropland. The United States loses about 33,000 acres (13,000 ha) of prairie potholes each year. (The actual number of acres drained varies, depending on drought conditions and economic factors.)

1

2

3

4

5

6

7

8

9

pull

Insert A

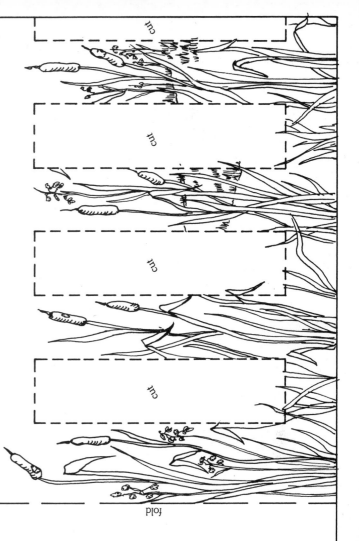

cut

cut

cut

cut

fold

pull

Insert B

43

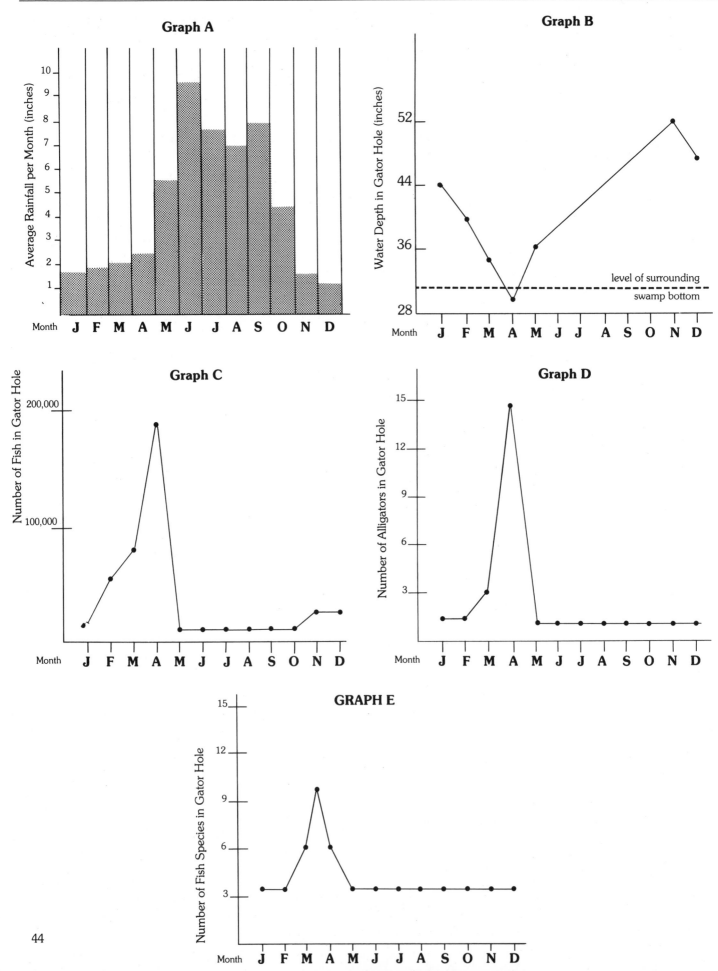

Graph A

Average Rainfall per Month (inches)

Month J F M A M J J A S O N D

Graph B

Water Depth in Gator Hole (inches)

level of surrounding
swamp bottom

Month J F M A M J J A S O N D

Graph C

Number of Fish in Gator Hole

200,000

100,000

Month J F M A M J J A S O N D

Graph D

Number of Alligators in Gator Hole

15

12

9

6

3

Month J F M A M J J A S O N D

GRAPH E

Number of Fish Species in Gator Hole

15

12

9

6

3

Month J F M A M J J A S O N D

1. According to Graph A, which month had the highest average rainfall? Which month had the least rainfall? In which months does the dry season occur?

2. According to Graph B, during which month did the water in the gator hole become lower than the surrounding ground?

3. According to Graph C, in which month was the number of fish in the gator hole highest?

4. According to Graphs A and E, did the greatest number of fish species occur in the gator hole during the wet season or the dry season?

5. Between which two months did the fish population decrease the most?
   a. April-May
   b. July-August
   c. January-February

6. True or false: According to Graphs B and D, the greatest number of alligators lived in the gator hole when the water depth reached 50 inches.

7. According to Graphs B and C, the fish population in the gator hole reached a peak when the water depth in the pond was at
   a. 52 inches
   b. 36 inches
   c. 30 inches

8. Raccoons, river otters, and many kinds of wading birds eat fish. Would you expect the numbers of these animals around the gator hole to increase or decrease during the dry season?

9. The wood stork, a fish-eating bird that lives in Big Cypress Swamp, will not lay eggs in years with very heavy rainfall. Why might this happen? Use the following information to form your answer.
   ● Wood storks nest high above the ground in the branches of bald cypress trees.
   ● Wood storks do not catch fish by looking for them—they feel for them. With their long beaks halfway open, the birds grope in the water for fish. When they touch their prey, their beaks instantly snap shut.
   ● To feed their young, the parents take turns flying to ponds, where they catch and swallow a large amount of fish. Then the adult flies back and regurgitates the partly digested fish into the nest for the young to eat. Until the babies are old enough to defend themselves, one parent always remains at the nest.

10. If the least rain fell in December, why was the level of water in the gator hole lowest in April?

WETLANDS, WILDLIFE, AND PEOPLE

What's a wetland worth? A lot! Just ask the people who live near the Everglades in southern Florida. Unfortunately, they've had to learn about the value of wetlands the hard way. The story of the Everglades is a good example of what has happened in other wetland areas across the country. In this chapter we'll take a look at how people and wetlands have interacted, using southern Florida as an example. We'll also discuss how wetlands, wildlife, and people depend on each other and what people are doing to help protect wetland areas.

THE EVERGLADES: A CASE STUDY
The Way It Was

As recently as a hundred years ago, water in Florida's Kissimmee River meandered south for about 100 miles (160 km), emptying into Lake Okeechobee. During wet years the lake flooded, washing Florida's southern tip—the Everglades—with a thin sheet of water. Slowly making its way south to the Gulf of Mexico, this wide film of water brought nutrients and water to millions of acres of rich sawgrass wetlands. Moving only about a foot a day, the water mixed with decaying sawgrass and other plant material, forming thick layers of peat and muck. And as the water trickled through the soil, it helped recharge the shallow aquifers that supplied the area with fresh drinking water.

The Everglades was a haven for wildlife, especially those species adapted to alternating wet and dry seasons. Wading birds nested in the sawgrass. Fish thrived on the billions of microscopic plants and animals that lived in the water. Deer fed on the lush vegetation, and raccoons, bears, and river otters hunted for fish and crayfish. Herons, egrets, wood storks, kites, and other wetland birds were common, as were alligators, snakes, and turtles.

Tipping the Balance

In the last hundred years, the delicate balance that existed between water, wildlife, and land began to collapse. To prevent flooding and create more "usable" land, engineers started tinkering with the Kissimmee River, Lake Okeechobee, and the Everglades. Canals were built and rivers were channeled to speed up water flow from the Kissimmee River to Lake Okeechobee and from Lake Okeechobee to the Gulf. And canals built south of Lake Okeechobee drained much of the Everglades' water into the Atlantic Ocean. This not only prevented flooding in many areas, but it also caused huge sections of the Everglades to dry up. Farmers planted thousands of acres of sugar cane and other crops on many of the once-thriving wetland areas. Other former wetland areas became pastures for livestock.

As southern Florida became more populated, development crept farther and farther into pristine wetland areas. More flood control measures were initiated, including the building of expensive channels, dikes, and diversions. Much of the rich peatland that had taken hundreds of years to form was drained and turned into farmland. Fertilizers from farms and lawns seeped into Lake Okeechobee, reducing the water quality of the lake.

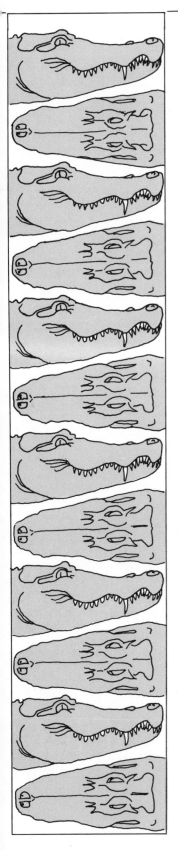

Water Out of Control

Finally the tinkering took its toll. The Everglades became too wet at times and too dry at other times. Uncontrollable fires raged across the land. Salt water began seeping into freshwater aquifers. And the loss of wildlife was great—from drowned fawns to wood storks that were unable to raise their young. With the water flow out of control and unpredictable, areas that were once gently washed with water were now either bone dry or completely flooded. Many biologists were concerned that the Everglades was so greatly altered that it would never function normally again.

Has the Tide Turned?

In the last few years, many people in southern Florida—including government officials—have gained a new respect for their valuable wetland systems. Instead of draining and filling wetland areas, Florida is now taking steps to turn the area back into what it once was by restoring the natural flow of water through the state. In a program called Save Our Everglades, federal, state, and local agencies, along with concerned citizens and private organizations, are working together to buy important wetland areas adjacent to the Everglades, to divert the Kissimmee River back closer to its original river channel, and to limit any future draining and channelization.

Wetland experts hope that the Save Our Everglades program will help turn back the clock so that by the year 2000 the Everglades will look more as it did in the 1800s.

WATCHING OUT FOR WETLANDS

Going, Going, Going: For an area that was once known as "wholly valueless," the Everglades seems to have gained the respect it deserves. But it and many other wetland areas are still facing serious problems. Since the first European settlers colonized North America, we have lost well over 50 percent of our wetlands. And we continue to lose between 300,000 and 500,000 acres (120,000 and 200,000 ha) of wetlands every year. Here are some other wetland areas that are in trouble:

- *Lower Mississippi Valley:* Only about 15 percent of the bottomland hardwood wetlands that once covered the lower Mississippi Valley still exist.
- *Prairie Potholes:* Only 5.3 million acres (2.1 million ha) remain of the 17 million acres (6.8 million ha) of prairie wetlands that once dotted North Dakota, South Dakota, and Minnesota. About 33,000 acres (13,000 ha) of prairie potholes continue to disappear each year.
- *Great Lakes:* Marshes along the Great Lakes have decreased 90 percent. These marshes not only provide habitat for fish and wildlife, but they also help to prevent shoreline erosion and minimize the destructive effects of storms.
- *California:* Less than 450,000 acres (180,000 ha) of California's original 5 million acres (2 million ha) of wetlands remain.
- *Iowa:* Less than 27,000 acres (11,000 ha) of wetlands remain in this state that once had over 2 million acres (800,000 ha).
- *North Carolina:* More than one-third of North Carolina's pocosin wetlands have already been destroyed and another 53 percent of the remaining pocosins in the state have been drained or cleared for future development.

(continued next page)

- *Connecticut:* Only one-half of Connecticut's original 30,000 acres (12,000 ha) of coastal marshes remain.

Taking Care of Wetlands: So what are we doing to help protect wetlands? From local zoning laws to state wetland acquisition to provisions in the national Clean Water Act, wetlands are starting to get protection at all levels of government. But due to lack of support and money, much of the legislation that has been passed to help protect wetlands is not enforced. And some of the legislation has been offset by conflicting legislation that encourages wetland destruction.

Two of the most effective wetland protection programs are the Duck Stamp program and Section 404 of the Clean Water Act. Both have helped save thousands of acres of critical wetland habitat. The Duck Stamp program, administered by the Fish and Wildlife Service, raises money to help buy valuable wetland habitats. (Waterfowl hunters over 16 years old are required to purchase a duck stamp annually. But anyone can purchase a duck stamp to help protect wetlands.) Section 404 of the Clean Water Act helps prevent wetland destruction through a carefully controlled permit program. Under guidelines established by the Environmental Protection Agency, the Army Corps of Engineers evaluates wetland projects, hears comments from citizens and private interest groups (as well as local, state, and federal agencies), and then decides whether or not to grant a permit to the developer. Section 404 does not prohibit wetland development. But if it is properly enforced, it does provide a way to control wetland destruction and encourage more ecologically sound alternatives.

Although these and other programs have given wetlands a helping hand, many conservation groups feel that much more wetland protection is needed, including tighter guidelines regulating wetland development. Many groups also feel the Army Corps of Engineers is not adequately enforcing Section 404. The National Wildlife Federation and other groups are working hard to establish a national wetland policy that would:

- prevent any additional loss of wetlands
- restore wetlands that have been dredged, drained and over-developed
- construct artificial wetlands as needed
- support wetland research
- strengthen existing wetland legislation

Don't Touch That Wetland: Although many of our farms and forests are former wetlands, people are now realizing that wetlands are most valuable as wetlands. They provide valuable wildlife habitat, offer peaceful retreats for hunters and hikers, provide special products from crawdads to cranberries, protect us from storm surges and floods, and filter pollutants. They also have the potential to clean up our waste. Artificial wetlands that can filter waste water are already in the operational stage, and many scientists feel that we will eventually be able to use specially designed wetlands as large scale wastewater treatment areas that filter pollution more efficiently and cheaply than traditional methods.

As more people become aware of the value of our wetlands and see the serious consequences that human tinkering can have, maybe we can avoid Everglades-type mistakes in the future. And maybe a new wetland awareness will erase the words *unproductive, wasteland,* and *worthless* from our wetland vocabulary and replace them forever with the words *productive, vital,* and *irreplaceable.*

1979 Duck Stamp

VOID AFTER JUNE 30, 1979

Hooded Merganser

U.S. DEPARTMENT OF THE INTERIOR

MIGRATORY BIRD HUNTING AND CONSERVATION STAMP

$5

From Marsh to Marina

Take a historical look at salt marshes and at the ways people have used them.

Objective:
Discuss some of the ways people have used and changed salt marshes through time.

Ages:
Primary and Intermediate

Materials:
- *copies of page 56*
- *pencils*
- *crayons or markers (optional)*
- *scissors*
- *glue*
- *large pieces of construction paper (one for each person)*

Subjects:
Science, History, and Social Studies

alt marshes can be great places to make a living! Native Americans living along the coasts knew this—and so did some of the earliest European settlers. Try this activity to get your kids thinking about how people have used (and abused) salt marshes over the years.

Begin by passing out copies of page 56. Explain that the pictures represent some of the ways people have used salt marshes through time. Have the kids cut out the pictures and then try to arrange them in order.

When everyone's finished, go over the answers. (See page 50. Each picture is lettered in the upper right-hand corner for easy reference.) Then have each of the kids glue the pictures in the correct order on a large sheet of construction paper. (You might want to have the kids color the pictures before they cut them out and glue them down.) Have them label the time period of each picture as follows:

Picture #1: 1600s
Picture #2: 1700s
Picture #3: early 1800s
Picture #4: late 1800s to early 1900s
Picture #5: 1950s
Picture #6: 1980s

Afterward, use the following information to talk about each picture.

SALT MARSHES THROUGH TIME

Picture 1: Native Americans were the first people to use the resources of salt marshes. In eastern North America, for example, the Delaware, Nanticoke, and Roanoke Indians hunted and fished in salt marshes. And in the West, the Miwok and Costanoan Indians depended on the salt marshes along the Pacific Coast.

The Indians found plenty of game in salt marshes—especially in the fall, when huge flocks of ducks and geese passed through during migration. Many of the Indians gathered oysters, clams, and other shellfish in the tidal creeks of salt marshes too. They also built special fish traps out of brush and scooped the trapped fish into baskets.

Pictures 2 and 3: Many Europeans settled near salt marshes during the 1700s and 1800s. Living near the marsh wasn't an easy life. For one thing, mosquitoes and other biting insects could be a terrible problem. And cattle would occasionally have to be destroyed when they sank too far down into the marsh mud to be rescued. But there were advantages to marsh living too. There was plenty of food, and the vast fields of salt marsh hay

made good grazing grounds.

Picture 4: By the late 1800s, many salt marshes in North America had been settled. In some marshes people began to have a big impact on the ecology of the land. Have the kids compare this situation with that depicted in Pictures 1 through 3. Explain that before there were so many people, the marsh could easily recover from the impact people had on it. But the more people that lived in a particular marsh, the more serious and long-lasting the damage that was done to it.

Ask the kids to name as many ways as they can think of that the people in this picture are affecting the marsh. Here are some things you can talk about:

- Before there were regulations on the hunting of shorebirds and other waterbirds, some species were hunted almost to extinction. Sandpipers and other salt marsh birds were hunted for their meat, and egrets and herons were killed for their feathers. (Their long, graceful plumes were used to decorate women's hats.)
- For years, many salt marshes and other wetlands were used as dumpsites for garbage.
- Since there were no regulations on the dumping of sewage during this time period, water pollution could be a problem in salt marshes near heavily populated areas. (Like all wetlands, salt marshes can tolerate a certain amount of sewage. But too much of it can turn a healthy marsh into a cesspool.)

Pictures 5 and 6: Point out that, by the 1950s, people had drastically changed many of the original salt marshes. Few people recognized the marshes' importance in their natural state. (See pages 18-20 and 46-48 for information about the value of wetlands to people and wildlife.) To turn them into "useful" places, they often filled them in and built airports, houses, and other buildings on them. Ask the kids to look at the first picture again, then ask them how the wildlife in the first and last pictures differs. (There are fewer kinds of animals in Picture 6. The animals that are present are only those species that can live close to people. And a few "non-marsh" animals such as pigeons and starlings have probably moved in. But herons, shorebirds, deer, and most of the other original salt marsh animals are gone.)

To wrap up your discussion, explain to the kids that there are now laws protecting salt marshes and other wetlands from unwise use. Some of these areas have been designated as wildlife sanctuaries. Ducks, geese, eagles, deer, fish, and many other animals depend on these areas—just as they did when Native Americans hunted and fished in them hundreds of years ago.

A trip to a salt marsh would be a great follow-up to this activity. See "Explore a Wetland" on page 8 for some tips and tricks you can use on a salt marsh field trip.

Answers: 1—D; 2—B; 3—F; 4—A; 5—C; 6—E

A Taste of Wetlands

Sample some tasty wetland foods.

Objectives:
Name some foods we get from wetlands. Discuss some ways people have used certain wetland plants through time.

Ages:
Primary, Intermediate, and Advanced

Next time you sit down to a Thanksgiving feast with all the trimmings, thank a wetland! Wetlands are responsible for a tasty part of most Thanksgiving meals: cranberries.

We have wetlands to thank for some other treats too. For example, certain kinds of mints grow in wetlands. So does wild rice. Wetlands also produce a lot of seafood, from oysters to shrimp to crabs to flounder. And many lesser-known foods grow in wetlands too. For example, did

you know that the roots, shoots, stalks, and even the pollen of cattails are edible?

Introduce your kids to some of the "incredible edibles" wetlands have to offer by trying some of these recipes. (You might want to have the kids make the recipes themselves, with your supervision. Each person could be responsible for bringing in an ingredient or utensil.) Use the information under "Did You Know?" to talk about each wetland "ingredient" as you taste your culinary creations.

Materials:
- plates and eating utensils
- ingredients and utensils for making wetland treats (see individual recipes)

Subjects:
Science and Social Studies

Cattail pollen pancake recipe reprinted from *Billy Joe Tatum's Wild Foods Cookbook and Field Guide* with permission from Workman Publishing Company, Inc.

Cranberries
- Wild cranberries grow in bogs and marshes. The cranberries people buy at the store are usually cultivated in specially prepared bogs in Massachusetts, New Jersey, Washington, Wisconsin, and other states.
- Early settlers called cranberry plants "crane berries" because they thought the pale pink cranberry blossoms looked like the head and neck of a crane. Later, "crane berry" got shortened to "cranberry."
- Cranberries are high in vitamin C. In the 1800s, sailors took the berries on long voyages and ate them to prevent scurvy.
- Indians ate cranberries and used them to make medicines and dyes.

Cattails
- Cattails grow in freshwater marshes and swamps.
- During World War I, cattail down (the fuzzy brown fluff from female flower heads) was used to make artificial silk.
- Indians used cattails in many ways. For example, they used the flowers to make soups, breads, and puddings, and they used the pollen to make breads. They also roasted and ate the seeds.

Mint
- There are more than 3000 different species of plants belonging to the group known as mints. Some of these plants aren't commonly known to be mints. For example, catnip, rosemary, and thyme are all mints.
- Many mints grow in freshwater marshes and along stream banks.
- Indians used mint medicinally. For example, some Indians fed their children a special mint tea to get rid of worms.
- Some mints are good sources of vitamins A and C.

Shrimp
- Many kinds of shrimp hatch at sea and then travel into salt marshes or mangrove swamps, where they grow to maturity.
- In the United States, shrimp is the most commercially valuable seafood. About three-quarters of the catch is harvested from the Gulf of Mexico.
- Some female shrimp can lay more than 500,000 eggs in less than five minutes.
- Some shrimp start their lives as males, then become females later.
- Some species of shrimp look more like tiny pears than shrimp when they hatch. They go through about 15 stages before they finally look like "real" shrimp.

[CAT]TAIL POLLEN [P]ANCAKES

- 1 cup cattail pollen (See the end of the recipe for directions on how to collect cattail pollen.)
- 1 cup flour
- 1 teaspoon baking soda
- ¾ teaspoon salt
- 2¼ cups buttermilk
- 2 tablespoons vegetable oil
- shortening or butter for frying

Sift together the cattail pollen, flour, soda, and salt. Stir together the buttermilk and oil. Add the liquid ingredients to the dry mixture, mix, and set the batter aside until it thickens (about 10 minutes). Cook the pancakes on a hot, greased griddle. (Makes about a dozen six-inch pancakes. Try folding some of them and filling them with jam, jelly, or whipped cream.)

Collecting cattail pollen: Cattails usually bloom from May through July. The pollen is bright yellow and forms on the male flower spikes, which grow up from the brown, fuzzy "sausages" of the female flower heads. To gather the pollen, just bend the cattail stalk over and shake the pollen into a bucket or bag. (Get permission from landowners or park officials before collecting cattail pollen.)

TANGY MINT TEA

- 1 cup dried mint leaves (spearmint or peppermint both work well)
- 1 quart boiling water
- 1 cinnamon stick
- honey

Crumble dried mint leaves into small pieces and add them to the boiling water. Boil for about a minute, then remove the tea from the heat and let it steep for 15 minutes. For the last five minutes of steeping, add a cinnamon stick. Strain into cups. Add honey to taste, and serve hot or cold. Makes about four cups of tea.

[E]XCEPTIONALLY EASY CRANBERRY MOLD

- 1 package raspberry gelatin
- 1 cup hot water
- 1 can cranberry sauce, "jelly style"
- 1 pint sour cream

Dissolve the gelatin in the hot water. Pour this mixture, along with the rest of the ingredients, into a blender. Blend until the mixture becomes frothy. Pour it into an oiled mold and chill until firm.

SPICY SHRIMP DIP

- 1 five-ounce package of cooked, frozen shrimp
- ½ cup sour cream
- ½ cup mayonnaise
- ¼ cup mild picante sauce
- 2 teaspoons lemon juice
- 1 teaspoon prepared horse radish
- dash pepper
- dash tabasco

Thaw the shrimp according to the directions on the package and cut them into small pieces. Mix them together with the rest of the ingredients, let chill, and serve with corn chips or crackers. Makes about 1½ cups of dip.

The Great Swamp Debate

Read and analyze two newspaper articles about a wetland issue.

Objectives:
Discuss the differences between two newspaper articles dealing with the same subject. Define biased. Discuss the controversy that surrounded the proposal to build an airport in the Great Swamp in the early 1960s.

Ages:
Intermediate and Advanced

Materials:
- *copies of page 57*
- *pens or pencils*
- *paper*
- *chalkboard or easel paper*

Subjects:
Science and Social Studies

S olving environmental problems isn't an easy job. In this activity your group will have a chance to see that, like all environmental issues, wetland issues can be very complex.

Before you start, copy the questions provided under "Analyzing the Articles" on a chalkboard or piece of easel paper. (Answers are on page 53.) Then pass out copies of page 57. Explain that the two articles on the page represent a real environmental controversy. The controversy began in 1959 when a transportation agency for New York and New Jersey, called the Port Authority, came up with a proposal to build a huge airport.

Tell the kids they'll find out later how the controversy was resolved. But first they'll be finding out more about it by reading the two articles you passed out and by answering some questions about them. Tell the kids that the articles aren't real, and neither are the quotes or names given in them. But the circumstances we've presented concerning the proposed airport, along with the controversy it raised, are true.

When everyone has finished reading the articles, tell the kids to draw a line down the middle of a blank sheet of paper. Have them write "Article 1" at the top of one column and "Article 2" at the top of the other. Then give them time to

answer the questions you wrote down. Explain that they'll be answering questions two, three, and four for both Article 1 and Article 2. (Questions one and five are a little different from the others. Have the kids answer these questions on the other side of their sheets.)

While you're going over the answers, discuss why it can be difficult for people to find out all the facts about an issue. One reason for this is that the news sometimes presents information in a *biased* way. Ask the kids if they know what the word *biased* means, then ask if they think either of the articles is biased. (Both are. Article 1 doesn't present any of the disadvantages of building the airport in the Great Swamp, and Article 2 doesn't present any of the advantages. That's not to say that the information presented in either of the articles is necessarily wrong—it's just incomplete.) But even though it may be difficult to know all of the facts, people still must make decisions—decisions that often affect other people, wildlife, and other natural resources. That's why it's important to try to find the least biased information available and to carefully consider all of the alternatives.

Now tell the kids what finally happened in the airport/Great Swamp controversy. Here's a synopsis:

The airport was never built. Instead, three nearby airports—Kennedy, LaGuardia, and Newark—were remodeled and/or expanded. The increased air travel that the Port Authority claimed would occur turned out to be not as dramatic as the figures predicted.

The Great Swamp Committee managed to raise enough money to buy the Great Swamp, and they donated it to the United States Government in 1964. It was established as a National Wildlife Refuge, National Natural Landmark, and Wilderness Area, which permanently protected it from development. Today it serves not only as a sanctuary for wildlife but also as a recreation area for bird watchers, hikers, nature photographers, and others. And biologists and other researchers use the Great Swamp as an outdoor "lab."

Aircraft Owners & Pilots Association (AOPA)

1. After reading the two articles, which of the following would you say is the main problem that needs to be solved?
   a. whether to build the airport in New York or in New Jersey
   b. whether or not the airport should be built in the Great Swamp
   c. how big the airport should be
   d. how far the airport should be from New York City

2. Does the article discuss any advantages of building the airport on the chosen site? If so, list them.

3. Does the article discuss any disadvantages of building the airport on the chosen site? If so, list them.

4. Which of the following attitudes does the article seem to have toward swamps?
   a. swamps are valuable in their natural state
   b. swamps aren't worth much in their natural state

5. Can you think of any compromises or alternatives to the issue of whether or not an airport should be built on the proposed site?

Answers:
1. b
2. *Article #1*—yes (would make a "useless swamp" useful to people; could help businesses grow, which would increase economic growth for Morris County; would create jobs); *Article #2*—no
3. *Article #1*—no; *Article #2*—yes (would be difficult and costly to develop the swamp; would increase pollution and noise levels; existing roads might not be able to handle the additional traffic; schools, houses, and other buildings might have to be destroyed; plants and animals would lose their habitat; the water supply in the area might suffer)
4. *Article #1*—b; *Article #2*—a
5. Other airports could be remodeled or enlarged; another site might be less costly and less environmentally damaging to develop; and so on.

freshwater marsh, Lake Erie

Alvin E. Staffan

What's Your Wetland IQ?

Play a wetland trivia game.

Objectives:
Describe several ways that wetlands are important to people and wildlife. Describe several ways people have abused wetlands.

Ages:
Intermediate and Advanced

Materials:
- *copies of page 58*
- *chalkboard or easel paper*
- *index cards*
- *crayons or markers*
- *glue*
- *scissors*
- *large sack*
- *paper (optional)*

Subjects:
Science, History, and Geography

 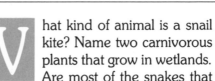

What kind of animal is a snail kite? Name two carnivorous plants that grow in wetlands. Are most of the snakes that live in swamps poisonous?

In this activity your group will get a chance to answer these and other wetland trivia questions by playing a team trivia game. At the same time they will learn more about how wetlands are important to people and wildlife.

Start the activity by asking the kids to describe ways that wetlands are important to people and to wildlife. List their answers on a chalkboard or large sheet of easel paper. Add to their list, using the background information on pages 3-4 and pages 46-48. Then tell the kids they are going to play a trivia game, but that first they each need to make a set of wetland cards.

Pass out a copy of page 58 to each person. Explain that each of the pictures on the top half of the page matches one of the clue cards on the bottom. Then see if the kids can find the matches. Discuss the answers, using the background information. (See answers at left.)

Next pass out index cards, crayons or markers, scissors, and glue and have each child turn his or her sheet into a set of game cards. First have them color the pictures and then cut out all of the rectangles on page 58 (pictures and clues). Tell them to glue each picture to a separate index card and then trim off the extra cardboard from the sides. Have them glue the matching set of clues to the other side of the picture card.

Each person can also make one wild card. (Wild cards will speed up the game.) Just have the kids glue blank paper to each side of an index card and write "wild card" on both sides.

When all the cards have been made, collect them in a large sack. Then divide the group into two teams. (You might want to give each team a few days to brush up on and review their wetland facts.) Explain that the object of "What's Your Wetland IQ?" is to be the first team to collect a complete set of wetland benefit cards—five in all. To get the cards, each team must correctly answer wetland trivia questions. (You might want to list the titles of the five wetland benefit cards on the board so the kids can keep track of what they need to win.) Here's how to play:

Have each team appoint a spokesperson. Then alternate from team to team, asking each a different trivia question from the list at the end of the activity. Explain that team members can discuss each question, but the answer must come from the spokesperson.

Each time a team correctly answers a question, one of the members gets to pick a card from the sack. If a team picks a wetland destruction card, the card should be put aside and the team must give up one of their other cards. (Don't put the destruction card back into the sack. If a team picks a wetland destruction card on the first round or before they have other cards, they just lose their turn.) There is no penalty for missing a question.

If you decide to use wild cards, explain that a wild card can replace any of the five wetland benefit cards. So if a team has all the cards but one and then picks a wild card, they win.

TRIVIA QUESTIONS

1. Name two kinds of freshwater wetlands. (swamp, freshwater marsh, bog)
2. Name three animals that might be found in a wetland. (frog, duck, fish, mosquito, beetle, spider, deer, beaver, muskrat, crab, snail, and so on)
3. Many carnivorous plants grow in wetlands. Name two. (sundew, pitcher plant, bladderwort, Venus flytrap, butterwort)
4. What term is used to describe the twice-daily rising and falling of seawater in a saltwater wetland? (tide)
5. Which fiddler crab has one claw many times larger than the other—the male or the female? (male)
6. True or false: If you go to a swamp you are likely to drown in quicksand. (False.)
7. What state is the Everglades in? (Florida)
8. What part of a bald cypress tree produces the tree's "knees"—the trunk, roots, or branches? (roots)
9. What is the most abundant tree growing in coastal saltwater swamps? (mangrove)
10. What is the name of the people, famous for their spicy cooking, who were driven out of Nova Scotia by the British in the mid 1700s and finally settled in Louisiana's bayous? (Cajuns)
11. What is the name of the plant that is grown in bogs and whose berries are harvested to make jellies for traditional Thanksgiving meals as well as to make breads, juices, and other foods? (cranberries)
12. Name a city in the United States that was built on a wetland. (Washington, D.C., Boston, San Francisco, and so on)
13. What bird is among the largest living birds, often builds its nest in mangrove trees, and feeds on fish which it catches in a huge pouch underneath its bill? (pelican)
14. Approximately what percentage of the commercial fish catch taken along the Atlantic and Gulf Coasts in the U.S. depends on wetlands for survival—25%, 50%, or 66%? (66%)
15. Along what three large bodies of water are the coastal saltwater wetlands of the United States located? (Gulf of Mexico, Atlantic Ocean, Pacific Ocean)
16. The Great Dismal Swamp is one of the largest swamps in the United States and stretches across the borders of two states. Name one of these states. (North Carolina or Virginia)
17. What wetland is often called a "river of grass"? (Everglades)

18. Name an endangered animal that lives in wetlands. (whooping crane, American crocodile, snail kite, Florida panther, red wolf, Pine Barrens tree frog, and so on)

19. "The land of the trembling earth" is the Indian name for a large swamp that is found in Georgia. The name of the swamp has five syllables and starts with the letter "O" What is this swamp? (the Okefenokee)

20. The skins of which wetland reptiles have been used by people to make purses, belts, and other accessories? (alligators and crocodiles)

21. Name two ways people abuse wetlands. (filling, dumping, dredging, draining)

22. The "quaking" movement of some bogs is caused by:
    a. small, localized earthquakes centered underneath the bogs
    b. the movement of underground water to the surface
    c. people walking or jumping on the thick layers of spongy peat
    (c is correct)

23. True or false: Most of the snakes that live in swamps are poisonous. (False)

alligator

Leonard Lee Rue III

24. True or false: There are wetlands in Israel. (True)

25. The dam-building practices of this mammal have helped create wetlands. What is its name? (beaver)

26. What advantage are prop roots to red mangroves? (The prop roots help give the trees support in unstable soil and are covered with lenticels through which oxygen passes.)

27. Is the wetland animal called a snail kite a snail, bird, or mammal? (a bird)

28. True or false: Male fiddler crabs make a strange, fiddlelike noise with their huge claws. (False. Male fiddler crabs use their big claws to defend their territories and to attract females.)

29. True or false: If it hadn't been for glaciers, many of the bogs in North America wouldn't be here today. (True. The glaciers that once covered much of North America gouged out basins that bogs later formed in.)

30. In what kind of wetland would you most likely find an American crocodile: a bog, a prairie pothole, or a mangrove swamp? (mangrove swamp)

31. True or false: In North America, mangrove swamps are most common in Canada. (False. Mangrove swamps are tropical wetlands. In North America, they're most common in southern Florida.)

32. True or false: A man who fell into a bog and died about 2000 years ago was found in the 1950s in an almost perfectly preserved state. He was even still wearing his hat! (True. Decomposition occurs very slowly in many bogs.)

33. Which of the following fish or shellfish doesn't depend on saltwater wetlands in some way: shrimp, tuna, oysters, or salmon? (tuna)

34. The menhaden is a commercially harvested fish that spends a lot of time in salt marshes. Which of the following products is *not* a big use of menhaden: fertilizer, paint, food, or soap? (food)

35. Which two states have the most acres of wetlands? (Alaska and Florida)

36. About what percent of endangered and threatened animals and plants in the United States depend on wetlands in some way: 10%, 35%, or 60%? (35%)

37. True or false: Some crabs live in mangrove trees and feed on their leaves. (True)

38. Which of the following agencies is in charge of giving permission to build on wetlands: the U.S. Fish and Wildlife Service, the U.S. Army Corps of Engineers, or the National Park Service? (the U.S. Army Corps of Engineers)

39. Which of the following is known for the huge numbers of ducks that are born there each year: the Potomac River, prairie potholes, or northern bogs? (prairie potholes)

40. Parts of what freshwater wetland plant have been made into flour for pancakes and stuffing for mattresses? (the cattail)

41. Many wetland areas have been drained, filled, or dredged. What does the word *dredge* mean? (to deepen a body of water by digging up the bottom)

42. Name two reasons that wetlands are often drained, filled, channelized, or dredged. (to create agricultural fields, marinas, parking lots, airports, dumps, and so on)

43. True or false: People can build artificial wetlands that can help filter pollution. (True)

44. Name a well-known swamp. (Dismal Swamp, Great Swamp, Okefenokee Swamp, Atchafalaya Swamp, and so on)

45. Which country in North America has the most bogs? (Canada)

46. Name a crop that is sometimes grown in wetlands. (wild rice, mint, cranberries)

47. Which of the following presidents gave an executive order to protect wetlands: Carter, Nixon, or Reagan? (Carter)

48. What do the bog turtle, whooping crane, and green pitcher plant have in common? (All live in wetlands, and all are endangered species.)

49. How much water can a brown pelican's pouch hold—½ gallon, 1 gallon, or 2 gallons or more? (2 gallons or more)

50. Spartina grass is the most abundant plant in which kind of wetland—a salt marsh, freshwater marsh, or bog? (salt marsh)

51. Sphagnum moss is one of the plants that grows in bogs. Although people have used sphagnum moss for many things, it has never been used for: fuel for heating houses, diapers, food, or wrappings for wounds. (food)

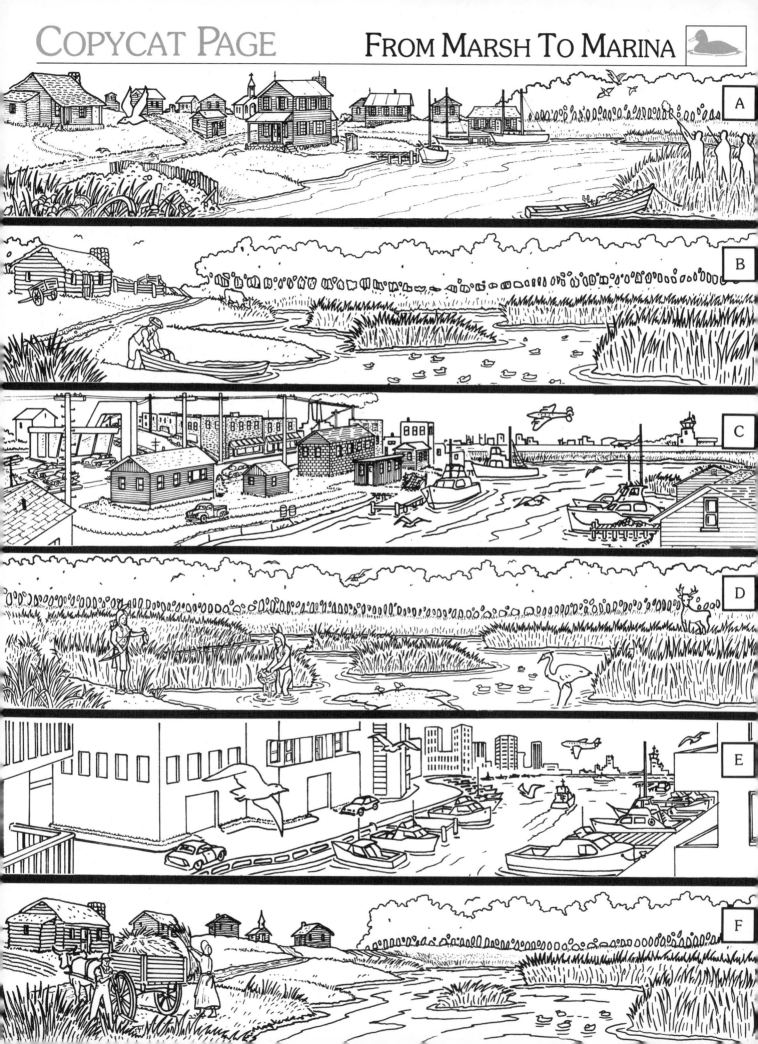

A

B

C

D

E

F

NEW AIRPORT NEEDED IN JERSEY

Aircraft Owners & Pilots Association (AOPA)

New York—The Port Authority, a transportation agency for New York and New Jersey, held a meeting here yesterday. The purpose of the meeting was to discuss plans for a new major airport to be built in the New York-New Jersey area. Ed Warren, a speaker for the Port Authority, explained that the airport will satisfy the growing need for more air travel services in the region.

The airport would need a large, level site, and one that's fairly close to New York City. "We've studied fifteen possible sites," said Warren, "and we think we've found the perfect location." Warren reported that the preferred site is in Morris County, New Jersey. "It's nothing but a big swamp right now, but it will be very useful to a lot of people once the airport gets underway."

Port Authority figures show that the other major airports in the area will soon have more business than they can handle. In the next five years, business is expected to double. And in fifteen years, it could increase by as much as three to four times its current level.

Discount store owner John Landis commented on the favorable effects the airport would have on stores, restaurants, and hotels located near it. "Our business will increase—no doubt about it," he said.

"And that means more economic growth for Morris County."

Labor leader Tom Hines agreed. "Thousands of new jobs will open up when building begins," he added. "There will be new opportunities for planners and construction workers. And once the airport opens there will be even more jobs. The airport will need ticket checkers, air traffic controllers, maintenance workers, and many, many others. Plus, the new airport will attract all kinds of new businesses around it."

Great Swamp IN DANGER

Morristown, New Jersey—Scientists, naturalists, and concerned citizens met here yesterday to discuss the plan for a new major airport to be built in the Great Swamp of Morris County. The purpose of the meeting was to discuss what can be done to prevent the building of the airport.

Sam Brown, a long-time resident of Morris County, presented facts from several scientific reports. "The reports indicate that building the airport in the Great Swamp will cause more problems than it will solve," he said. According to the reports, the swamp area would be very difficult and costly to develop. "It's going to cost a lot of money to drain out the swamp water and keep it out," Brown said.

Increased noise and pollution to communities near the swamp were cited as other problems that the airport would cause. Many people also feel that existing roads will not be able to handle the added traffic to and from New York.

Tina Shore, another Morris County resident, pointed out that many homes, churches, and schools near the proposed airport site would probably have to be destroyed to make way for the huge airport. "It would affect thousands of people," she said. "And it might affect the water supply in the area."

University biology professor Judy Dayton talked about the history and biology of the Great Swamp. "The swamp is left over from the last Ice Age, when the area was part of a glacial lake. It's home to many plants and animals," Dayton explained. "Building the airport here would destroy their special habitat. And many wouldn't be able to adapt to new surroundings."

"I grew up with the swamp as my playground," said Allen Jones, a local high school student. "The Great Swamp has a lot to teach us all," he added.

WHAT'S YOUR WETLAND IQ?

FLOOD CONTROL

RECREATION

HABITAT FOR WILDLIFE

POLLUTION CONTROL

POLLUTION

PREVENT SOIL EROSION

WETLAND DESTRUCTION

- wetlands trap silt
- some wetland plants can filter pollutants from water
- many wetland plants can absorb some pollutants as nutrients

A

- wetlands provide food, water, shelter, and living space for many types of wildlife
- many birds, fish, amphibians, and other animals lay their eggs in wetlands
- salt marshes, mangrove swamps, and other wetlands act as natural nurseries for many types of wildlife

B

- roots of wetland plants help bind soil
- wetland vegetation and soils help slow runoff from storms and melting snow
- wetlands help protect shorelines by slowing down the waves and water currents

C

- people alter and abuse wetlands by dredging, dumping, channelizing, filling, and draining
- altered wetlands often become farmland, housing sites, marinas, grazing land, highways, and other developed areas

D

- wetlands provide opportunities for canoeing, bird watching, fishing, hunting, photography, and hiking
- wetlands often inspire painters, writers, poets, and others

E

- wetlands help soak up rain and melting snow
- some wetlands can temporarily store storm waters
- wetlands often help contain flood waters and slow them down

F

CRAFTY CORNER

Cattails for Kids

Make cattails using felt and pipe cleaners.

Ages:
Primary

Materials:
- brown felt
- long pipe cleaners
- green construction paper
- glue
- scissors
- tape
- copies of cattail "head" pattern

Subjects:
Arts and Crafts

Your kids can make cattails that look like the real thing! But before they start, make some cattail "heads" for them to work with. Just trace the pattern piece shown below onto brown felt, making sure you trace two patterns for each child. Then cut out the pieces and hand them out. (You might want to have older kids trace and cut out their own cattail heads.)

Provide green construction paper and long pipe cleaners, then have the kids follow these steps:

1. Put glue on one side of a felt piece, making sure you spread it evenly and fairly thickly over the whole side. (Don't rub the glue into the felt! If you do, the felt will become too sticky and wet to work with.)
2. Lay a pipe cleaner lengthwise along the middle of the glue-covered felt, leaving about one inch (2.5 cm) sticking over the top edge (see diagram). Now lay the other felt piece on top. Press the two together firmly and let them dry.
3. Cut long, tapering leaves out of green construction paper. (Two or three leaves are enough for one cattail.) Fold the bottom of each leaf around the pipe cleaner stem, then tape them in place (see diagram). Your cattail is now complete!

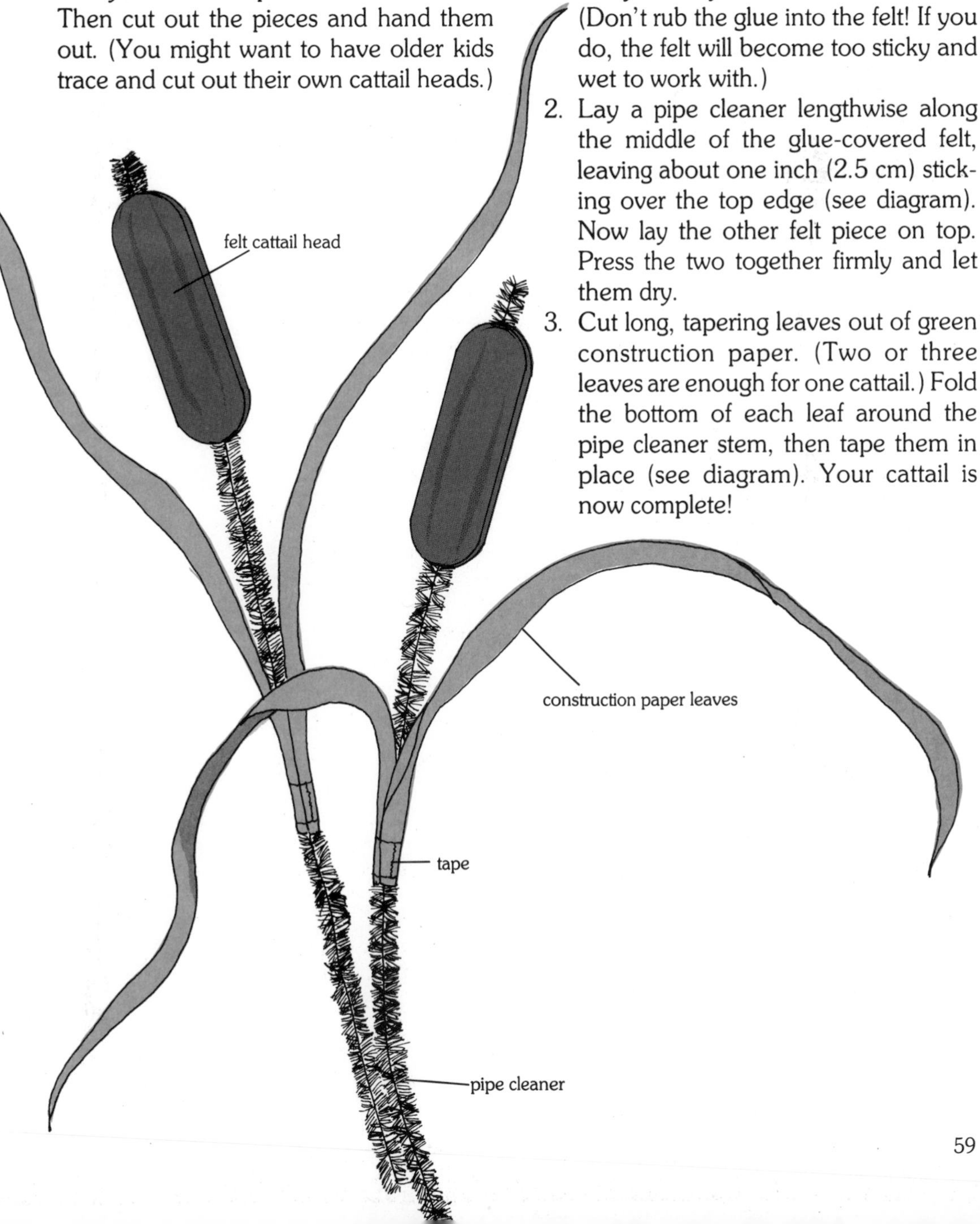

felt cattail head

cattail head pattern

construction paper leaves

tape

pipe cleaner

This Pitcher's a Catcher!

Make a pitcher plant that really catches flies.

Ages:
Intermediate and Advanced

Materials:
- copies of the pitcher plant pattern and fly pictures
- thin cardboard (about the thickness of a file folder)
- cardboard
- ¾ × 4" (2 × 10-cm) strips of paper (three per person)
- 11" (28-cm) pieces of string
- scissors
- pencils
- glue
- tape
- crayons or markers
- pictures of pitcher plants

Subjects:
Arts and Crafts

Here's a great way for your kids to learn about pitcher plants—those incredible "meat-eating monsters" that grow in bogs and marshes. First lead a brief discussion about how and why pitcher plants and some other plants "eat" insects. (See "Little Green Monsters" on pages 36-37 for background information.) Show the kids pictures of pitcher plants as you talk.

Then give each child a copy of the pitcher plant pattern and fly pictures shown on the next page. Now have them make their own fly-catching pitcher plants, following these directions:

1. Trace the pitcher plant pattern onto a piece of thin cardboard and cut it out.
2. Color both sides of the cut-out. (Have the kids refer to pictures of pitcher plants so they can color them accurately.)
3. Roll the cut-out into a cone (see diagram below). Tape the outside edge to hold the cone together.
4. Glue one of the fly pictures to a small piece of cardboard, then cut it out along the solid black line. (If the kids want to color their flies, have them do it before gluing them to the cardboard.)
5. Glue one end of the string to the other side of the cardboard. Then cut out the second fly picture and glue it over the string.
6. To make the downward-pointing hairs that line the insides of pitcher plants, fold the strips of paper in half lengthwise. Then cut diagonal slits in one half of each strip (see diagram).
7. Apply a line of glue to the uncut side of each strip and carefully glue the "hairs" to the inside of the cone (see diagram). Make sure that the hairs point *down*, toward the base of the cone. Repeat for the other two strips. (You might want to use a pencil to guide the hairs in place.)
8. Tape the loose end of the string to the inside front lip of the pitcher plant (see diagram).
9. Curl the "hood" by rolling it around a finger and holding it in place for a moment.

Now the pitcher plants are ready to catch flies! Have the kids try flipping the flies into the pitchers. With a little practice they can make their "meat-eating monsters" catch insect meals over and over again!

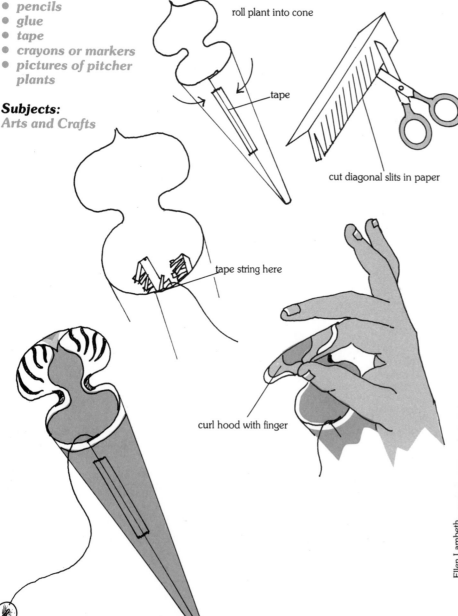

roll plant into cone

tape

cut diagonal slits in paper

tape string here

curl hood with finger

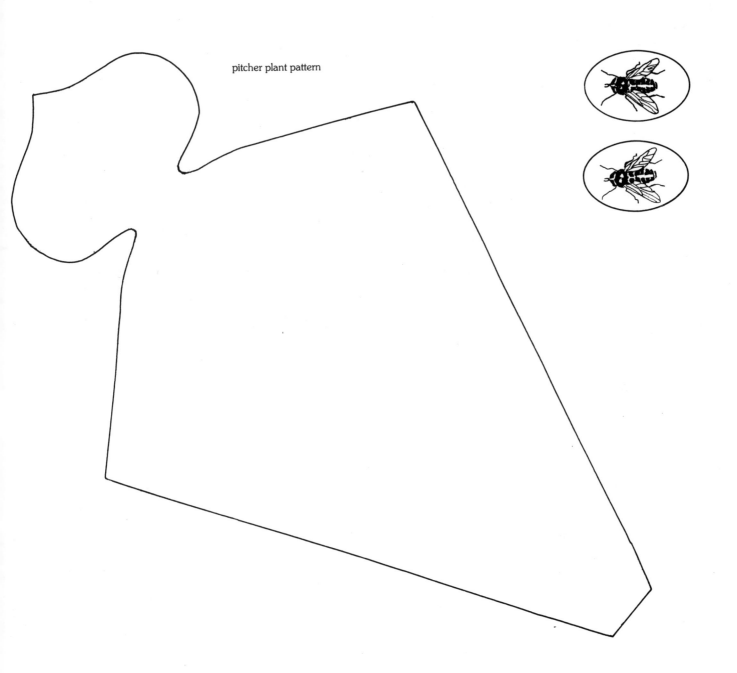

pitcher plant pattern

Wild Wetland Critters

Create stand-up wet-land creatures using cardboard, construction paper, and markers.

Ages:
Intermediate and Advanced

(continued next page)

Have your kids make their own menagerie of wetland wildlife! Just pass out thin cardboard, paper, and other art supplies, and let them follow these directions:
1. Draw the animals on drawing paper or construction paper and color them.

2. Glue the drawings onto thin cardboard and let them dry.
3. Before cutting your animals out, read "Finishing Touches" (on the next page) and look at the drawings we've provided for ideas on how to make them stand up and move.

(continued next page)

Materials:
- drawing paper or construction paper
- thin cardboard
- scissors
- crayons or markers
- glue
- paper fasteners (optional)

Subjects:
Arts and Crafts

FINISHING TOUCHES

- To make a long-legged wetland bird or other wetland critter stand up, make a simple stand for it. First cut a base around the animal's legs or undersides, as shown. Make a slit in the center of the base. Then cut a crosspiece out of thin cardboard and cut a slit in its center too (see diagram). Push the crosspiece through the base at the slits and adjust the stand so that your animal stands up.
- You can put a little action into your wetland critters by attaching separate body parts with paper fasteners. The shorebird we've pictured, for example, can stand straight up or bend over to find food in the water. (Its body and legs are separate pieces, held together with a paper fastener.)
- Some creatures, such as the crab and alligator we've pictured, don't need stands. Just bend the animals' legs down and let them stand on their own!
- Try bending other parts of your animals to give them more of a three-dimensional look. For example, we've bent the dragonfly's wings slightly to make them stand out. You can also tape or glue on other body parts, such as an alligator's lower jaw and its mouthful of teeth.

When the kids have finished making their animals, you might want to have them make wetland dioramas to put the animals in.

paper fastener

bend wings out

bend legs down

cut slit in base and in crosspiece
fit together to make a stand

APPENDIX

Canada goose

Alvin E. Staffan

Glossary

bogs—poorly drained freshwater wetlands that are characterized by a build-up of peat. Sphagnum mosses are found in many bogs.

channelization—the process of changing and straightening the natural path of a waterway. Channelization is often used as a means of flood control, but its negative effects often outweigh its advantages. For example, channelization often damages wetlands associated with rivers and streams.

detritus—bits of vegetation, animal remains, and other organic material that form the base of food chains in wetlands and many other kinds of habitats.

dredging—the process of digging up and removing material from wetlands or from the bottoms of waterways to clear them or make them deeper or wider. For example, tidal creeks in salt marshes are often dredged to make them wide enough for boat passage. Dredging and activities associated with it can damage wetlands.

freshwater marshes—open wetlands that occur along rivers and lakes, and in many other areas. Sedges, reeds, rushes, and grasses are the dominant plants in freshwater marshes.

freshwater swamps—forested or shrubby wetlands. Pocosins and heaths are two examples of freshwater swamps.

lenticels—tiny pores, into which oxygen passes, on the roots or branches of trees. For example, both red and black mangrove trees have lenticels on some of their roots.

mangrove swamps—saltwater wetlands that occur along tropical coasts. Mangrove trees are the dominant plants in mangrove swamps.

peat—partially decomposed plants and other organic material that builds up in poorly drained wetland habitats. Thick, compressed layers of peat are characteristic of many bogs.

pneumatophores—small, sticklike roots of black mangrove trees that grow up from the mud. Pneumatophores are covered with lenticels and absorb oxygen from the air.

prairie pothole region—an area stretching from the Midwest into Canada that's scattered with deep and shallow marshes and wet meadows. Millions of ducks and other animals depend on prairie potholes as feeding, nesting, and resting sites.

prop roots—long, tangled roots of red mangrove trees that grow down from the trees' trunks and branches. Prop roots give red mangroves support, and they're covered with lenticels.

salinity—the concentration of salt in an area. The salinity of a saltwater wetland changes whenever it rains and each time the tide rises and falls.

salt marshes—saltwater wetlands that occur along many coasts north and south of the tropics. Spartina grasses are the dominant vegetation in many salt marshes.

sediment—particles of sand, soil, and minerals that are washed from the land and settle on the bottoms of wetlands and other aquatic habitats.

tidal flats—saltwater wetlands that are characterized by mud and/or sand. Tidal flats often occur at the seaward edges of salt marshes. They're covered with seawater during high tide and become exposed during low tide. Algae are the dominant plants in tidal flats.

wetlands—areas that, at least periodically, have waterlogged soils or are covered with a relatively shallow layer of water. Wetlands support plants and animals that are adapted to living in a watery environment. Bogs, freshwater and saltwater marshes, and freshwater and saltwater swamps are examples of wetlands.

Bibliography

(Note: A [image] at the end of a listing indicates that a book is a good source of wetland pictures.)

GENERAL REFERENCE BOOKS

Atchafalaya: America's Largest River Basin Swamp by C.C. Lockwood (Beauregard, 1982) [image]

Atlantic Beaches, The Bayous, The Everglades, Northeast Coast, and *The Okefenokee Swamp* are part of a series called *The American Wilderness* by the editors of Time-Life Books (Time-Life, 1973) [image]

Exploring Our Baylands by Diane Conradson, Ph.D. (Coastal Parks Assn., 1982) (focuses on San Francisco Bay area and its wetlands)

Freshwater Marshes—Ecology and Wildlife Management by Milton W. Weller (University of Minnesota Press, 1981)

The Life of the Marsh by William A. Niering (McGraw-Hill, 1966) [image]

The Living Swamp by A. Borgioli and G. Cappelli (Orbis, 1979)

Status Report on Our Nation's Wetlands by J. Scott Feierabend and John M. Zelazny (National Wildlife Federation, 1987)

The Water Naturalist by Heather Angel and Pat Wolseley (Facts on File, 1982)

Waterlogged Wealth by Edward Maltby (Earthscan, 1986)

FIELD GUIDES

Audubon Society Nature Guides: Atlantic & Gulf Coasts by William H. and Stephen H. Amos (Knopf, 1985) [image]

Audubon Society Nature Guides: Pacific Coast by Bayard H. McConnaughey and Evelyn McConnaughey (Knopf, 1985) [image]

Audubon Society Nature Guides: Wetlands by William A. Niering (Knopf, 1985) [image]

Life in and around Freshwater Wetlands by Michael J. Ursin (Crowell, 1975)

A Sierra Club Naturalist's Guide: The Middle Atlantic Coast, Cape Hatteras to Cape Cod by Bill Perry (Sierra Club Books, 1985)

A Sierra Club Naturalist's Guide: The North Atlantic Coast, Cape Cod to Newfoundland by Michael and Deborah Berrill (Sierra Club Books, 1981)

CHILDREN'S BOOKS

Alligator by Jack Denton Scott (Putnam, 1984). Primary and Intermediate

Alligators by Ada and Frank Graham (Delacorte, 1979). Advanced

Between Cattails by Terry Tempest Williams (Scribner's, 1985). Primary and Intermediate

The Cranberry Book by Elizabeth Gemming (Coward-McCann, 1983). Advanced

Dragonflies by Oxford Scientific Films (Putnam, 1982). Primary and Intermediate [image]

Estuaries: Where Rivers Meet the Sea by Laurence Pringle (Macmillan, 1973). Intermediate

The Everglades: Exploring the Unknown by Christopher Linn (Troll, 1976). Primary

Explore a Spooky Swamp by Wendy W. Cortesi (National Geographic Society, 1976). Primary [image]

Exploring the Bayous by John L. Tveten (David McKay, 1979). Advanced

The First Book of Swamps and Marshes by Frances C. Smith (Franklin Watts, 1969). Intermediate

Mosquito by Oxford Scientific Films (Putnam, 1982). Primary and Intermediate [image]

Swamp Spring by Carol and Donald Carrick (Macmillan, 1969). Primary

A Walk through the Marsh by C. William Harrison (Reilly and Lee, 1972). Intermediate

Wetlands: Bogs, Marshes, and Swamps by Lewis Buck (Parent's Magazine Press, 1974). Primary

Where the Waves Break: Life at the Edge of the Sea by Anita Malnig (Carolrhoda, 1985). Intermediate and Advanced

Year on Muskrat Marsh by Berniece Freschet (Scribner's, 1974). Primary

FILMS, FILMSTRIPS, RECORDS, SLIDE SETS, AND VIDEOS

Bog Ecology, Ecology of a Bog, The Salt Marsh Biome, Ecology of the Everglades, Ecology of a Swamp, and *Freshwater and Salt Marshes* (All Ages) are slide sets with accompanying teacher's guides. *Salt Marshes—A Special Resource* (Intermediate) is a set of two filmstrips with teacher's guide. For ordering information write to Educational Images Ltd., P.O. Box 3456, West Side, Elmira, NY 14905.

Conserving America: Wetlands (Advanced) is a video with accompanying activity and resource guide. Videos and a limited supply of guides are available from the National Wildlife Federation, 1400 16th St., NW, Washington, DC 20036-2266.

The Marsh Community (Primary and Intermediate) and *Our Vanishing Marshland* (Advanced) are available in film or video from Encyclopaedia Britannica Educational Corp., 425 N. Michigan Ave., Chicago, IL 60611.

Romp in the Swamp is a record (or cassette) of 14 upbeat kids' songs by Billy B. (Bill Brennan). Jenson Publications, P.O. Box 248, New Berlin, WI 53151-0248 Attn: Sales Department.

A Swamp Ecosystem (Advanced) is available in film or video from National Geographic Society, Educational Services, Dept. 89, Washington, DC 20036.

BOOKLETS, KITS, MAPS, AND POSTERS

Energy Flow in a Wetland is a poster with a board game format, including game rules and background information. For more information, write to the National Science Teachers Association, 1742 Connecticut Ave., NW, Washington, DC 20009.

Life at the Seashore (Intermediate) is a *Wonders of Learning Kit* containing 30 student booklets, ready-to-copy activity sheets, teacher's guide, and read-along cassette. Order from National Geographic Society, Educational Services, Dept. 89, Washington, DC 20036.

Natural Florida has colorful posters of swamps; rivers and flood plains; and mangroves and salt marshes. The posters focus on Florida but are good general references. For ordering information write Tropical Nature Services, Rt. 1, Box 860, Micanopy, FL 32667.

Salt Marshes—Food for the Sea is a booklet on food chains. For more information write to the Massachusetts Audubon Society, Public Information Office, Lincoln, MA 01773.

U.S. Government Printing Office has a poster of the Everglades (stock number 024-005-00487-4). For a catalog with this and other posters, write to Superintendent of Documents, U.S. Government Printing Office, Washington, DC 20402.

Virginia Coast Reserve Coloring Book is available from the Nature Conservancy, 1800 N. Kent St., Arlington, VA 22209.

Wavelets are free fact sheets with background information on marine topics. Wetlands sheets include salt marshes, brackish marshes, and freshwater wetlands. To order write Sea Grant Communications, Virginia Institute of Marine Science, Gloucester Point, VA 23062.

Wetlands Adoption Kit contains background information and tips on how to help preserve wetlands. For more information write Izaak Walton League of America, 1401 Wilson Blvd., Level B, Arlington, VA 22209.

OTHER ACTIVITY SOURCES

Coastal Ecosystems (Primary) is an activity unit containing a teacher's guide; student field guides on salt marshes, sandy beaches, piers and jetties, and mud flats; plus instructions on setting up a saltwater aquarium. Also available are "Coastal Livelihoods and Crafts" (Advanced), "A Guide to Field Studies for the Coastal Environment" (Advanced), and others. For a catalog write Project CAPE, Dare County Schools, P.O. Box 817, Manteo, NC 27954.

Elkhorn Slough National Estuarine Research Reserve has an extensive curriculum packet for elementary educators. Contains background information, ready-to-copy pages, and activities on estuaries, sloughs, and marshes. Also available is a teaching kit on wetland birds called "Bird Adaptations/Beaks and Feet." Write Elkhorn Slough National Estuarine Research Reserve, Attn: Education Coordinator, 1700 Elkhorn Rd., Watsonville, CA 95076.

The Estuary Book (Advanced) is an activity guide with background information, detailed illustrations, and activities from the British Columbia Teachers' Federation. For a catalog write B.C. Teachers' Federation, Lesson Aids Service, 2235 Burrard St., Vancouver, BC V6J 3H9.

The Estuary Program (All Ages) contains background information, field and classroom activities, and ready-to-copy activities. For information write Padilla Bay National Estuarine Research Reserve, 1043 Bayview-Edison Rd., Mt Vernon, WA 98273.

Estuary Study Program (Intermediate and Advanced) contains background information and activities on estuaries. For information write South Slough National Estuarine Research Reserve, P.O. Box 5417, Charleston, OR 97420.

Marine Education—A Bibliography of Educational Materials Available from the Nation's Sea Grant College Programs includes wetland-related publications available from Sea Grant College Programs in the United States. For information write to Texas A&M University, Sea Grant College Program, College Station, TX 77843-4115.

The U.S. Fish and Wildlife Service has developed activity guides on Estuaries, Freshwater Marshes, and Tidal Marshes. Also available is an issue pac on Wetland Conservation and Uses. These guides contain posters, activity sheets, lesson plans, and background information. Most are suitable for primary through advanced kids. For information write National Institute for Urban Wildlife, 10921 Trotting Ridge Way, Columbia, MD 21044.

Wetlands Are Wonderlands (Advanced) contains teacher and student activity guides on freshwater wetlands. Sponsored by the Illinois/Indiana Sea Grant Program. To order a complimentary set write Illinois/Indiana Sea Grant Program, University of Illinois, 65 Mumford Hall, 1301 W. Gregory Dr., Urbana, IL 61801.

SOFTWARE

Yaker Environmental Systems offers two wetland-related programs for Apple computers. *Estuaries: The Ocean's Nurseries* (Advanced) teaches about estuaries and the animals that live there. *Biomes II: Wilderness Webs* (Advanced) allows children to build food webs in eight different biomes including the Everglades. For information write Yaker Environmental Systems, Inc., P.O. Box 18, Stanton, NJ 08885.

WHERE TO GET MORE INFORMATION

- federal and state departments of parks, game and fish, natural resources, and wildlife
- local chapters of the Audubon Society, Ducks Unlimited, and the Izaak Walton League
- museums and nature centers
- state and local college and university departments of biology, ecology, and environmental science
- wildlife refuges

Ranger Rick Wetland Index

Ranger Rick, published by the National Wildlife Federation, is a monthly nature magazine for elementary-age children.

Adventures of Ranger Rick, Oct 76, p 20 (wetlands)
Adventures of Ranger Rick, Mar 78, p 18 (swamp)
Adventures of Ranger Rick, Sep 80, p 28 (swamp)
Adventures of Ranger Rick, Feb 86, p 42 (Big Cypress Swamp)
Adventures of Ranger Rick, May 87, p 8 (saving wetlands)
Adventures of Ranger Rick, May 89, p 38 (how beavers help create wetlands)
The Alligator Case, Mar 78, p 37
The American Alligator, May-Jun 69, p 4
Beaver Bother, Jun 88, p 14
Bird City, Jan 71, p 4 (swamp birds)
Caring for Crocs, Feb 82, p 18
Catchy Word Find, Aug 88, p 21 (pitcher plant game)
Cattail Caterpillars, Nov 80, p 34
Cattail Floats, Jul 80, p 38 (craft)
Cattails, Mar 76, p 12
The Cranes Are Dancing, Jul 74, p 28
Everglades Adventure, May-Jun 71, p 16
Gators and Crocs, Nov 78, p 24
The Ghost of Wilson Swamp, Oct 85, p 28 (swamp gas)
Goodbye Fly! Aug 87, p 36 (cobra plants)
How the Marshmallow Got Its Name, Jul 79, p 13
Land of the Trembling Earth, Oct 68, p 4 (Okefenokee)
Life in a Cypress Swamp, Jul 72, p 24

Look Out for Charley! Apr 79, p 29 (red-winged blackbird)
Muskrat Marsh, Jan 79, p 21
Musquash, the Muskrat, Oct 68, p 44
Mystery in the Marsh, Feb 88, p 8
Mystery Marsh, Aug-Sep 76, p 20
Nature Did It First, Oct 82, p 36 (Venus flytrap)
The Not-So-Barren Pine Barrens, Dec 72, p 42
Okefenokee is OK by Me, Aug 82, p 22
One Big Bullfrog, May 89, p 42
Our Coasts, Special Issue, Aug 80
Plants That Eat Animals, Nov 77, p 26
Problems of Parents, Aug 88, p 18 (stilts)
Return of the Spoonbill, Apr 72, p 44
Save Our Wetlands, Mar 76, p 32
Search for the Everglade Kites, Jul 80, p 41
Seaside Hide-and-Go-Seekers, Aug 82, p 36 (animals of bays and marshes)
Skunk Cabbage, Feb 67, p 44
Trees That Walk, Nov 86, p 38 (mangroves)
Trees With Knees, Jul 72, p 20 (bald cypress)
Trouble on the Coast, Aug 80, p 8
The Turtle Grass Community, Feb 72, p 19
Where the Rivers Meet the Sea, Nov 71, p 25

1997 UPDATE

TABLE OF CONTENTS

THE KISSIMMEE RIVER COMES HOME.................................69

by Sandra Chisholm-Robinson

- The Calusa
- The Seminole
- More And More Settlers
- Trying To Tame The Waters
- Wetlands Versus Safety
- Restoring The River
- Restoring The Everglades
- The New Everglades
- The Challenge Of Restoration
- Hope For Tomorrow

PRAIRIE MAGIC...73

by Dan R. Limmer

- A Biologist Looks Back
- Early Spring Adventures
- Zooplankton
- Intruder In A Watery World
- "Magical" Transformations
- Stories In The Mud
- Courtship In The Sloughs
- Summer Shifts
- Busy Times In The Wetlands
- Winter Wetlands Wonderland
- The End Of Prairie Magic?

URBAN WETLANDS..78

by John Quinn

- Where Or When?
- Separate Worlds, Side By Side

- Nearly Destroyed By "Improvements"
- Worth More Than A Passing Glance
- A Great Wall Of Ice
- A Distant Time
- The Great Lake Drains
- The First Europeans
- Urban Sprawl
- The Hackensack Meadowlands Development Commission
- Protecting And Preserving The Meadowlands
- Walking A Tightrope
- Trade-Offs: Are They Worth It?
- What's Your Position?

WETLANDS & WAL-MART...83

by Pamela Selbert

Bibliography Update...87

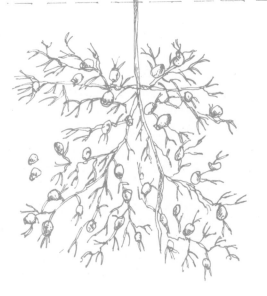

horned bladderwort

water level

THE KISSIMMEE RIVER COMES HOME

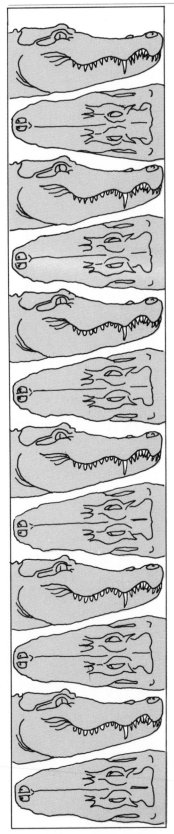

by Sandra Chisholm-Robinson

The Calusa

Bronze-skinned, with long black hair, a Calusa poled his cypress canoe up the river Kissimmee (kuh-SEH-mee), or "Long Water." He carried pottery, shells, and bone ornaments to trade for flint and copper. He followed the river north. He saw black bears feeding on palmetto berries and deer grazing in the marshes. The green tree tops turned white as thousands of birds—ibis and egrets—roosted on the branches. Ducks settled in great flocks on the wetlands created by the river. As the evening grew cooler, alligators slid silently into the warmer water from their sunning places on the riverbanks. A red wolf howled in the distance. The river provided for all of them—the bear, the birds, the alligator, the wolf, the man.

The Seminole

Many years after the Calusa became extinct, the Seminole people also followed the winding Kissimmee River. They said it was carved by a big snake that crawled down the center of the Florida peninsula to Lake Okeechobee (O-kee-CHO-bee). The Seminole moved south to the "River of Grass," or the Everglades, to escape enemy soldiers who pursued them.

During the time of the Seminole, water flowed through the Kissimmee River into Lake Okeechobee, or "Plenty Big Water." Water spilled over the southern rim of the lake and spread in a thin sheet throughout the Everglades. It finally drained into estuaries, smaller bodies of water which in turn flowed into Florida Bay. Here, fresh water mixed with the salt water of the bay in just the right amounts to create a nursery where young fish, shrimp, and crabs could grow.

More And More Settlers

After fighting three wars to maintain their freedom, the surviving Seminole made their homes in the Everglades. European settlers also built their houses on the banks of the Kissimmee River. Steamboats traveled up and down the river to bring flour, salt, guns, and bullets to the homesteaders in exchange for deer meat, alligator hides, and other animal skins. Over the years, more and more people built their homes and businesses near the river and around Lake Kissimmee, from which it flowed.

Trying To Tame The Waters

But even though people tamed the land, the river would not be tamed. In some seasons, the sky boiled with black clouds that blocked out the sun. Wind blew with a terrible force, and rain fell in sheets. The "Long Water" overflowed its banks. Homes and buildings were flooded; lives were lost.

Many people said the river must be controlled. So, in the years between 1960 and 1971, huge dredges burrowed across the land. The winding, 102-mile river that flooded and fed thousands of acres of wetlands was forced between deep, high banks. Now it was no longer the winding, twisting Kissimmee. Now it was a deep, straight 56-mile canal with a new shape and a new name: C-38.

In the years when water overflowed the banks of the Kissimmee River during the rainy season, it soaked the marshes where ducks and other water birds rested and fed. But when the water was confined within the deep walls of C-38, the wetlands dried up. Most of the birds did not return. The deep waters of the canal could not provide for the fish as the river had. Soon there were fewer and smaller fish for birds, otters, and people to catch.

fiddler crab

Wetlands Versus Safety

Many people were disturbed. They wanted to be safe from the floodwaters, but they missed the birds, the fish, the river, and the wetlands the river supported. They asked the water managers whether it was possible to restore the Kissimmee River—to let it flow again through its old twisting, winding banks.

So the water managers put dirt back into about 23 miles of the middle section of C-38. They hoped this would force the water back into the abandoned bends of the Kissimmee River. They hoped it would bring back 43 miles of river channel and 26,500 acres of wetlands in just the right places—where the floodwaters wouldn't harm people's homes or businesses. They hoped that more than 300 wildlife species, including several endangered ones, would benefit. But would it work?

Restoring The River

When engineers did a test in one small part of C-38, the water flowed back to its old banks. Soon, the rains and the river brought natural floodwaters back to the wetlands. The river returned home. So did the plants and animals that needed the marshes to survive.

Restoring the Kissimmee River is the largest project of its kind in the world. It will require about $300 million, over 50 million tons of dirt, and 15 years to complete. The plans also include improving the quality of water flowing into the Everglades, not just the quantity. More than 40,000 acres of wetlands will be reconstructed, containing cattails and other marsh plants that help remove pollutants from storm water runoff before it flows into the Everglades.

Restoring The Everglades

The Kissimmee River project is one of many restoration efforts in southern Florida. The Everglades is a wetland that once covered four million acres and stretched from Lake Okeechobee to Florida Bay. Today, it is half that size and in serious trouble. As more and more people moved to southern Florida, canals and flood-control structures were built to drain the Everglades and to manage flooding. When the natural flow of water was interrupted and sometimes stopped completely, wetland plants and animals suffered. Some species became endangered.

Scientists and water managers who studied the Everglades for several years discovered that it is not just a matter of getting water to the Everglades, but getting *clean* water delivered in the right amount, at the right time, in the right way.

The New Everglades

But restoring the Everglades does not mean turning back the clock to that "lost world" of over one hundred years ago. Today, more than five million people live in southern Florida. They share the wetlands with alligators, wood storks, and saw grass. It is now impossible to restore the Everglades to the way it was a century ago. In fact, many scientists think that would not be right. They say we should look forward to the twenty-first century—toward creating a new Everglades that will be different from the old, yet retain some of the wildness and diversity it once had.

The Challenge Of Restoration

Restoration is no easy task. Imagine if someone smashed a clock, then told you to put it back together so that it would keep time perfectly as it once did. You have no idea what the clock looked like before it was damaged. You are not even sure how to make the many separate pieces work together again. Restoration in the natural world is even more difficult. Since changes happened many years ago, important parts are now missing. Our knowledge of the original Kissimmee River, Lake Okeechobee, and the Everglades is incomplete and may be lost forever.

Hope For Tomorrow

As many scientists, engineers, citizens, and government agencies work together to restore the Everglades, there is a feeling of hope in southern Florida. As the river and wetlands return home, so can the plants and animals that live in them.

As we learn more about the environment and how we have changed it, there will be more restoration projects around the world. Who knows? Someday you may have the knowledge, skill, and caring to help restore a wetland. Perhaps some day you will help a river return home.

PRAIRIE MAGIC

by. Dan R. Limmer

 oung boys and girls are always looking for adventure, and I was no different. I found it in the wetlands on our farm in eastern South Dakota. These potholes, or "sloughs" (SLEWS) as we called them, could be found both on the croplands and in the pastures.

There are hundreds of thousands of these small, shallow prairie potholes, or ponds, scattered across the upper midwestern United States. Each is several feet deep and only a few acres across. They formed about 11,000 years ago when slow-moving glaciers scooped out soil and rocks. They dry up in late summer, but for most of the year these shallow bowls are full of rainwater or melted snow and ice. All year round, when I was a boy, they offered places for magical expeditions limited only by my own imagination.

A Biologist Looks Back

I know now that all these firsthand experiences of "prairie magic" convinced me to become a biologist when I grew up. I went to college and earned a degree in wildlife management, with a special concentration on wetlands and waterfowl. I have since learned and discovered scientific explanations for all the "magical" things I observed as a young boy. Yet I find that these things are no less interesting or magical because they have scientific explanations.

One of the most important things I have learned is how fortunate we all are to have these valuable natural resources. I have discovered that the pothole wetlands play a critical role in the life cycles of many wildlife species, especially waterfowl. Pothole wetlands act as important purifiers of our water supplies. They also hold back or slow down floodwaters. And they give pleasing variation to the landscape. I know now that they are valuable to people who have never had the pleasure of wandering the wetlands the way I did as a boy.

Early Spring Adventures

Early each spring, I built mighty rafts by nailing together wooden fence posts as floats and using scrap lumber as decking. Runoff waters from the melting snow would flow into the wetlands, creating a whole new world to explore after the cold, barren days of winter lost their grip on the land. With my long push-pole in hand, I was ready to launch my raft on voyages into unknown frontiers. And even though the snow and ice often lingered in these cool, early spring days, the sloughs were already alive with thousands, maybe millions, of "water bugs."

Zooplankton

Years later, I would learn that these tiny animals were invertebrates called *zooplankton*. Invertebrates are animals without skeletons. Zooplankton are a large group of invertebrates. Although zooplankton are usually very small, they are very high in protein. This makes the tiny invertebrates an important "main dish" for migrating and nesting ducks, especially when the ground is still frozen. Although the ducks might find some leftover grain scattered in the fields, this plentiful "duck soup" provides important energy and nutrients they need for the long trips during migration, and for laying and hatching their eggs later in the spring.

Intruder In A Watery World

As I poled my raft through the marshes, muskrats swam through the cattails and bulrushes. They always kept a careful eye on me. If I came too close, they would dive under the water and disappear into one of their many "houses" constructed of floating piles of wetland vegetation. These aquative animals hadn't seen the light of day for up to five months since retreating to their watery homes when the wetland froze the fall before. I always imagined that they were swimming around just for the fun of it after a long, dull winter cooped up inside.

Years later, I would learn that muskrats perform a very important task in the wetland. They are primarily vegetarians. By feeding on cattails, bulrushes, and other aquatic plants—or by using them to build houses—muskrats create areas of open water which are very important to wetlands wildlife. Without the muskrats, the sloughs would soon be choked with vegetation and become less welcoming to the waterfowl and wildlife.

"Magical" Transformations

It was nothing less than magic to watch the sloughs change in only a few days from frozen whiteness to a world teeming with ducks, geese, blackbirds, egrets, and herons. The antics of these birds were always peculiar and often comical. I later learned what their actions meant, and came to appreciate the immense diversity and complexity of nature.

By late spring and early summer, the sloughs came even more alive with the sounds of courting frogs, ducks, Canada geese, red-wing and yellow-headed blackbirds, and dozens of other species. At this time of year, the wetlands teemed with activity as they offered homes to many forms of wildlife.

Stories In The Mud

Each day I'd wait anxiously for school to end so I could rush home, finish my chores as quickly as possible, then set out on another adventure in the sloughs. I could hardly wait to discover what animals had wandered into the wetland the night before. Tracks in the mud and muck along the edges of the potholes told me that a mink or raccoon had hunted quietly in search of a tasty frog. Sometimes I'd find the tracks of a meandering skunk, or the prints of a great blue heron stalking the wetland habitat for a meal.

Courtship In The Sloughs

The birds of the wetlands fascinated me most of all. The number of different types of ducks that use pothole wetlands is incredible. Each year I was amazed to watch the courtship, or mating rituals, of the birds. In each case, the males competed for the privilege of pairing and mating with the females. Their courtships took place in the air and on the water and were different for different species.

For the mallards, a dozen or more drakes (males) performed astounding flying stunts as they competed for the attention of one hen (a female). When they landed on the water, they continued to compete for attention by dipping their bills in the water, quickly twisting and turning their heads, and preening—smoothing their beautiful feathers with their beaks.

Canada geese perform their own special courtship rituals in the air and on the water. Then, when a mated pair claims a nesting site, they use loud honking to defend their nest and the entire area around it. They'll even push away intruders if they have to.

The yellow-headed and red-wing blackbirds also have their very own courtship behavior. The males arrive in the wetland before the females. Each male chooses his territory. From then on, he defends it aggressively as he flies from perch to perch around the outer edges of his claim, singing and displaying his feathers. The females arrive one to two weeks later. After choosing a mate, the female begins to build their nest.

As a boy, I wondered why the wetlands waterfowl behaved this way. My studies help me understand. There are more males than females in waterfowl species. In order to mate, the drakes must successfully attract a hen and discourage other male rivals. The special courtship behavior also insures that the birds pair and mate with another of their own species.

Summer Shifts

As summer came to the farm, the wetlands in the pastures and croplands quickly changed again. The cattails and bulrushes grew tall in the warmer weather. Great swarms of biting insects often made my expeditions uncomfortable. But it was well worth it when I'd catch glimpses of a new brood of ducklings paddling across the water. My views were always cut short as the hen quickly led her young into the thick vegetation for safety. The ducklings could actually run across the water as they instinctively followed their mother to cover.

I learned later that even the insects which sometimes made my trips so miserable were important as sources of food for the young ducklings. For the first week or two of their lives, the tiny ducklings fed almost entirely on the wetland insects.

Busy Times In The Wetlands

Late summer and early fall were busy times on our farm. With the first frost came the harvest of crops and a sense of urgency to prepare for the coming winter. I thought I could also observe a sense of urgency in the way the wildlife began to behave. The muskrats began to build new houses or make additions to older ones. The ducks formed larger flocks and began to fly together into the fields to feed. Early each morning, thousands of blackbirds flew up out of the cattails where they roosted at night. Their flocks formed long, winding lines that looked like smoke rising from a chimney.

Later, my training as a biologist taught me that my observations as a boy were correct. The wetlands animals were getting ready for the long winter ahead, just as we humans were by harvesting our crops. Some animals prepared food and shelter to keep them through the long, cold northern winter. Others prepared to migrate south to warmer regions until spring came again.

Winter Wetlands Wonderland

Late in the year, when the wetlands froze and the winter snows started to fall, my young farmboy's prairie "magic" seemed to act in reverse. The prairie became much quieter—almost as if a spell of silence fell over the wetlands along with the snow. The noisy flocks of migrating ducks and birds were gone. The muskrats were tucked inside their houses among the cattails, which looked like igloos under their cover of snow. Other animals sought shelter from the cold in their own special ways.

But not all was quiet on the frozen sloughs. The cattails and bulrushes provided critical shelter from the prairie blizzards for pheasants and deer. I could easily trail them through the cattails. And if I looked closely, I might even find the tracks of a fox on the prowl or a hungry mink that had left its warm den in search of a meal.

The End Of Prairie Magic?

Our wetlands are critically important to our wildlife—and to all of us. Yet our nation has lost over half of its original 200 million acres of wetlands. Most of this loss occurred over the last hundred years because of urban development, highway construction, industrial expansion, and agriculture.

What will happen to all the wildlife that depends on the wetlands for food and shelter? What will happen to the wetlands waterfowl and wildlife if their prairie potholes are turned into crop fields or parking lots? Where will they go? How will they survive? And how can we survive their loss?

Those long-ago prairie winters on our farm were cold and long, but I spent those nights thinking about the coming spring and looking forward to the magical transformation that would occur again as it had for thousands and thousands of years. I know that my expeditions to the sloughs—and the "magic" I found there—led me to become a wetlands biologist. I will always be grateful for the inspiration I found in the prairie wetlands. If we all work in our own way to understand and preserve wetlands, we can help prairie magic continue on for many thousands of years to come.

URBAN WETLANDS

by John Quinn

Our canoe glides silently up the narrow, winding creek. Its bow slips between banks lined with lush green reeds twelve feet high. There are no sounds except the rush of wind in the reeds and the calls of invisible birds. A flock of gulls rides the warm air currents up into the blue sky. A small brown mammal slips into the water and swims quickly across our path. Hundreds of little fish nose about near the banks, creating tiny ripples in the water. As the canoe rounds another bend, we startle a beautiful, pure white bird. It leaps from the river bank, rises swiftly into the wind, and flaps away.

Where Or When?

We are enjoying an outdoor adventure that could have taken place hundreds or even thousands of years ago, because this coastal marsh has existed for more than twenty centuries. Wetlands creatures like the ones we see—the gulls, the muskrat, the fishes, and the snowy egret—have lived in this marsh for a very long time.

This scene could be unfolding before us in a marshy wilderness far from civilization. But, in fact, we are quite near one of the largest cities in the world. This marsh has changed dramatically over the past three centuries. As we paddle out of the small creek and into the main river that flows through the marsh, these changes become obvious. The silence of the reeds is suddenly overwhelmed by the low but constant roar of traffic that rushes over a busy, eight-lane superhighway cutting through the heart of the wetland. A jumbo jet thunders overhead on its way to the busy international airport just south of the marsh. The southern horizon is broken by electric transmission towers and their webs of wires. Even more spectacular, the hazy skyline of a great city rises above the marsh grasses to the east. The entire surrounding landscape is covered with buildings, power lines, and smoke stacks. Nearly all of the land encircling this marshland is covered by the factories, highways, and homes of millions of people.

Separate Worlds, Side By Side

This large urban wetland is now known as the Hackensack Meadowlands. It is a 20,000-acre "urban wilderness" located just six miles from New York City in one of the most densely populated areas of North America. Here, two separate and very different worlds exist almost side by side. In the reedy creeks and wide mudflats of these wetlands, we can see what the wilderness looked like when Europeans first arrived here in the early 1600s. But if we glance to the east, we can see the world-famous Manhattan skyline, with the tall spires of the Empire State Building and the World Trade Center—great towering symbols of the world of today and tomorrow.

Nearly Destroyed By "Improvements"

The Hackensack Meadowlands of today is a completely urban wetland that was nearly destroyed by the nearby metropolitan area. Over the past 300 years, the marsh has been threatened over and over again by efforts to "improve" it. The wetlands have been drained for agriculture and mosquito control. Many hundreds of acres were used for garbage and trash disposal or filled with thousands of tons of concrete from demolished buildings. Until very recently, no one gave any thought to how this affected the sensitive coastal marine ecosystem—the complex web of animal and plant life that grew in the marshes. To most people, the Meadowlands were nothing but a forbidding and useless wasteland, fit only to be "reclaimed"—put to use as sites of industry and housing. Environmental damage occurred so swiftly and was so complete during the twentieth century that by the early 1960s only one-third of the original marshland remained.

Worth More Than A Passing Glance

Most people know these wetlands as the sprawling Meadowlands Sports Complex and Giants Stadium. Millions of travelers glance at these grassy plains when they whiz through them on their way to or from New York City. They wrinkle their noses at the foul smells that pollute the air and water. But of course, these are not the "real" Meadowlands. To learn the true identity of this urban wetland and how it came to be, we must travel back in time more than 12,000 years.

A Great Wall Of Ice

It is the end of the Pleistocene period of Earth's history. A giant glacier called the Wisconsin Ice Sheet covers all of Canada and much of the northern United States. In what will someday be the state of New Jersey, the ice—3,000 feet deep in places—extends to a point just south of today's Manhattan Island. Where the great ice wall ends, there is a 50- to 300-foot-high rim of boulders, gravel, and stones.

About 12,000 years ago, the glacier receded as it melted away. Its meltwaters—melted ice water—backed up behind the giant rim of rocks and gravel to form several huge but shallow lakes. One of these was the icy-cold Glacial Lake Hackensack.

A Distant Time

Glacial Lake Hackensack existed for about 2,000 years. In this distant time, great beasts—woolly mammoths, mastodons with 8-foot tusks, and giant ground sloths—lived in North America. At about the same time, the very first Native Americans arrived in the eastern part of our continent. They probably knew both the wide, icy lake and the creatures that once prowled its shores.

hooded pitcher plant

The Great Lake Drains

Between 9,000 and 10,000 years ago, the glacial lake finally drained away, leaving its 15-mile-wide bed bare and empty. Only the winding, slow-flowing Hackensack River—called the "River of Many Bends" by the first Americans—remained in the old lake valley. Over the centuries, plants gradually reclaimed, or grew back in, the empty lake bed. By the time the first Dutch and English settlers arrived, the ancient lake had been replaced by wide marshes and extensive cedar forests.

The First Europeans

The first Europeans found marshes and lowland forests teeming with a wonderful variety of plant and animal life. Unfortunately, they did not view it as land with any real value. They viewed the wetlands as a wasteland—nothing more than an obstacle to their orderly settlement of the new land. They called the marshes "meadows" not because of the way they looked, but because of what they planned to do—drain them and turn them into more "useful" meadows for cattle and crops. When those Dutch farmers dug the first narrow drainage ditches in the mid-1600s, they began to transform the Meadowlands into the urban wetlands of today.

Urban Sprawl

By the mid-twentieth century, urban sprawl—rapid, unplanned growth from nearby cities—completely surrounded and even invaded this marsh. But the wetlands were still home to many species of fishes, birds, and mammals. Highways and railroads criss-crossed the meadows. Landfills, or garbage dumps, covered hundreds of acres. Pollution poisoned the river and air. Still, the healing powers of the marsh were not totally destroyed. Life persisted here—but for how much longer? By the 1960s, only about 8,000 acres of undeveloped wetland remained out of the original 20,000 acres—and there were growing pressures to fill in and develop the rest.

The Hackensack Meadowlands Development Commission

By 1968, some people—including members of the New Jersey state legislature—were concerned enough about the fate of this urban wetland to try to end the destruction. They formed a state agency called the Hackensack Meadowlands Development Commission, or HMDC. It was ordered to create and carry out plans to stop garbage dumping, control further development, and take steps to protect the remaining natural marsh habitat. At this time, the old Dutch "meadows" were renamed the Meadowlands.

Protecting And Preserving The Meadowlands

Since 1969, the HMDC has made several plans to develop and protect the Meadowlands. This is not an easy task, as much of the land is privately owned. And because they are part of a large urban area that needs land to keep growing, the wetlands are also extremely valuable as real estate for new homes or industries. A century ago, one acre of the meadows often sold for one dollar. Today, one acre of undeveloped marsh may be worth $50,000 to $100,000.

Walking A Tightrope

Today the HMDC walks a tightrope between environmentalists—who insist that no more marsh should be destroyed—and developers, who want to reclaim and develop the land to provide jobs and services for people in the New York–New Jersey metropolitan area. The HMDC introduced the Special Area Management Plan, or SAMP. It calls for thousands of acres of healthy marsh to be preserved—kept in their present state. Other degraded, or unhealthy areas, either will be restored to their original state or filled and developed. The cost of this restoration would be paid by the property owners and developers who are given the go-ahead to develop their land.

Trade-Offs: Are They Worth It?

As might be expected, most environmentalists oppose the SAMP development and preservation proposals. They insist that since so much of the "real" meadowlands already have been lost to development and pollution, any further filling and building will destroy them completely. On the other hand, developers are eager to meet the needs of the growing metropolitan area and to make money.

What's Your Position?

The debate over the future of the Meadowlands is one that is—or will soon be—taking place in many other urban areas. How should planners weigh the interests of people against the value of the wetlands? To what extent should we prevent people from building on this valuable land? How far should we go to protect these ecosystems?

What do you think?

WETLANDS & WAL-MART

by Pamela Selbert

ason Spanel, 14, loves woods and wetlands, but that's not too surprising—he has spent much of his young life learning about them from his father, Mike Spanel, a wildlife biologist for the Shawnee National Forest in southern Illinois.

What makes the high-school freshman honor student from Eldorado, Illinois, unusual is his intense interest in preserving the environment and his desire to "take back" abused land. Jason's efforts have resulted in the establishment of the J. L. Markham Wetland Restoration and Interpretive Site. The project turned a muddy 3.6-acre temporary water-retention basin adjoining a Wal-Mart parking lot into a flourishing wetland where 100 different types of plants grow and a dozen bird species make their home. The Wal-Mart store is in Arrowhead Point shopping center in Harrisburg, about seven miles west of Eldorado.

Jason Spanel (above) *plants wetland grasses amid a dusty parking-lot runoff area and* (left) *ends up with a full-fledged wetland and a boardwalk.*

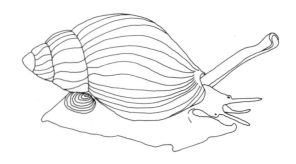

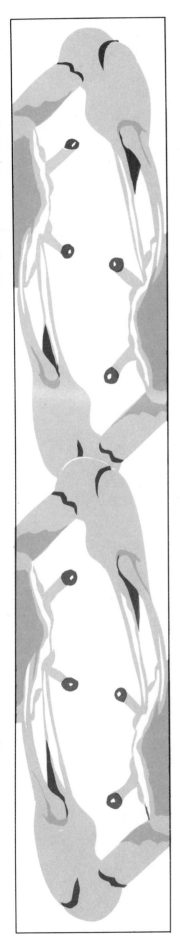

"The spillway for the parking lot lay right along the highway, and it was a mess—bare mud with trash all around," said Jason, whose scout uniform is peppered with badges, including the 50-Mile award, Arrow of Light, and Snorkeling. "My first thought was how much better it would be for the shopping center's business if something nice were there instead." The area seemed "perfect for a wetland, maybe even with bird boxes and a nature trail, where people driving by could stop for a look—it might even attract some shoppers to the center," he added.

Jason, a member of Eldorado Boy Scout Troop 137, was then hoping to become an Eagle Scout, the organization's highest rank, and he needed a project. Developing a wetland seemed like a "great project" and his father offered to suggest appropriate plants.

"I went to talk with the Wal-Mart manager, Tim Henson," said Jason, "and he said I'd have to contact the shopping center developer, Joseph Markham."

The letter to Markham was the first of what turned into a major paperwork operation—more than 200 letters, now photocopied and assembled in a thick binder along with the responses.

"Mr. Markham agreed to turn me loose," said Jason. "My dad challenged me to be creative and think big, and to think of all kinds of ways to accomplish my goal."

Henson suggested that Jason apply for a grant from the Wal-Mart Foundation to help with funding. Within a few weeks a check for $350 had arrived. Since then, donations from a variety of sources increased his funds for the wetland to $2,000.

"Besides the cash, other help had come from many different areas," Jason said. About 50 groups and individuals—garden clubs and greenhouses from around the country, local scout troops, a TV station, sawmill, concrete plant, an artist, the U.S. Forest Service, and many others—received a letter of request from Jason and have provided labor, advertising, and resources for the project.

A local landscape architect helped Jason develop a plan for the moist-soil wetland, the Illinois Department of Conservation and a nursery in Tennessee donated more than 300 trees needed to "reforest" the area, and a nursery in Wisconsin contributed 100 native moist-soil plants for ground cover.

On Arbor Day, April 7, 1992, Jason directed the wetland planting. His father, brother Chris, 15, and sister Laura, 8, plus scouts from Eldorado Troop 137 and Harrisburg Troop 23, helped with the work. Harrisburg Mayor John Cummins and State Representative David Phelps were on hand for the occasion.

So people will be able to learn about the wetland without having to walk in the mud or damage the fragile soil, Jason has completed a boardwalk with interpretive signs to guide them. Jason's future plans for his wetland include a gazebo on the boardwalk and constructing an interpretive trail.

Although he has devoted many hours to his wetland project, Jason has not let it slow him down. He received an all-expense-paid trip to Washington, DC, to accept a $7,500 award for an essay he submitted to the American Express

Geography Essay Contest. At the Tri-State Regional Science Fair in Evansville, Indiana, Jason won the Kodak award for photography. And he also won five days at Space Camp at the U.S. Space Academy in Huntsville, Alabama.

But among all these accomplishments, his wetland will live on well after he has grown and moved on with his life. It will remain as an example of one young person's dedication to the environment and a willingness to help others learn about an important aspect of nature.

Beth Shimp, a forest botanist from the Shawnee National Forest, said, "People are enjoying Jason's wetland, watching the changes that take place with the different seasons. I think one thing he's accomplished here is to dispel the bad image wetlands traditionally have had as nothing more than mosquito breeders—in fact, they clean water as it comes through."

"With many thousands of acres of wetlands being drained every year," said Jason, "it's important for people to recognize their value before they're completely gone."

Jason Spanel became the youngest recipient of a grant from the North American Wetlands Conservation Fund when he received a symbolic $600 check from Mollie Beattie, director of the U.S. Fish and Wildlife Service in Washington, DC. FWS' Acting Assistant Director, William Hartwig (far left), and Steve Poole, Jason's teacher, were also there to witness the May event.

Bibliography Update

Note: A * at the end of a listing indicates that the book is a good source of wetland pictures.

GENERAL REFERENCE BOOKS

Bogs of the Northeast by Charles W. Johnson (University Press of New England, 1985)

The Field Guide to Wildlife Habitats of the Eastern United States by Janine M. Benyus (Simon & Schuster, 1989)

Freshwater Marshes: Ecology and Wildlife Management by Milton W. Weller (University of Minnesota Press, 1994)

Pond and Brook: A Guide to Nature in Freshwater Environments by Michael J. Caduto (University Press of New England, 1990)

Wetlands of North America by Bates Littlehales and William A. Niering (Thomasson-Grant, 1991)

FIELD GUIDES

Pond Life (Golden Guide) by George K. Reid (Golden, 1987) *

Pond Watchers Guide to Ponds and Vernal Pools of Eastern North America (Massachusetts Audubon Society, 1996) *

Sierra Club Naturalist's Guides: The North Woods of Michigan, Wisconsin, Minnesota & Southern Ontario by Glenda Daniel and Jerry Sullivan (Sierra Club Books, 1981)

Sierra Club Naturalist's Guides: Southern New England by Neil Jorgensen (Sierra Club Books, 1978)

CHILDREN'S BOOKS

Everglades by Jean Craighead George (Harper Collins, 1995). Primary *

Pond (One Small Square® series) by Donald M. Silver (McGraw-Hill, 1997). Intermediate

Pond Life (Look Closer series) by Barbara Taylor (Dorling Kindersley, 1992). Advanced *

Pond & River (Eyewitness Book series) by Steve Parker (Knopf, 1988). Advanced *

Saving Our Wetlands & Their Wildlife by Karen Liptak (Franklin Watts, 1991). Advanced

Squish! A Wetland Walk by Nancy Luenn (Atheneum, 1994). Primary

Squishy, Misty, Damp & Muddy: The In-Between World of Wetlands by Molly Cone (Sierra Club, 1996). Primary *

Swamp Life (Look Closer series) by Jane Burton and Kim Taylor (Dorling Kindersley, 1993). Advanced *

Wetlands Nature Search by Andrew Langley (Joshua Morris/Reader's Digest, 1993). Intermediate *

VIDEOS, FILMSTRIPS, AND SLIDES

Bog Ecology, *Ecology of a Bog*, *The Salt Marsh Biome*, *Ecology of the Everglades*, *Freshwater and Salt Marshes*, *Ecology of a Swamp*, and *Salt Marshes* (All Ages) are slide sets, filmstrips or videos with teacher's guides. For ordering information write to:
Educational Images Ltd.
Box 3456 W
Elmira, NY 14905
U.S.A.

Conserving America: Wetlands (Advanced) is a video. For information write to:
V.I.E.W. Video
34 E. 23rd St.
NY, NY 10010
U.S.A.

Let's Explore a Wetland (Intermediate) is a video and teacher's guide. For a catalogue write to:
National Geographic Society
Educational Services
P.O. Box 98019
Washington DC 20090-8019
U.S.A.

Our Vanishing Marshland (Advanced) is a video. For information write to:
Encyclopedia Britannica Educational Corp.
310 S. Michigan Ave.
Chicago, IL 60604-9839
U.S.A.

Secrets of the Salt Marsh (Intermediate and Advanced) is a video with study guide and activities. For information write to:
Bullfrog Films
Box 149
Oley, PA 19547
U.S.A.

Swamp and Marsh (Primary and Intermediate) is a video with teacher's guide. For information write to:
SVE
6677 N. Northwest Hwy.
Chicago, IL 60631
U.S.A.

A Swamp Ecosystem (Advanced) is a video. For a catalogue write to:

National Geographic Society
Educational Services
P.O. Box 98019
Washington, DC 20090-8019
U.S.A.

Swamp Survival Ecosystem (from Ecology: Interrelationships in Nature series) (Intermediate and Advanced) is a filmstrip, cassette, and script. For information write to:
SVE
6677 N. Northwest Hwy.
Chicago, IL 60631
U.S.A.

The Wetlands (Primary to Advanced) is a video and discussion guide. For information write to:
AIMS Media
9710 DeSoto Ave.
Chatsworth, CA 91311
U.S.A.

BOOKLETS, POSTERS, FACT SHEETS, AND GAMES

Energy Flow in a Wetland is a poster with a board-game format, including game rules and background information. For information write to:
National Science Teachers Association
1840 Wilson Blvd.
Arlington, VA 22201-3000
U.S.A.

Herons, Frogs, and Cranberry Bogs: A Wetlands Unit for Science and Language Arts (Advanced) is a student activity text and teacher's guide on fresh and saltwater wetlands, including 28 lessons, experiments, use of field guides, maps and diagrams, and neighborhood wetland investigation. For information write to:
J. Weston Walch
P.O. Box 658
Portland, ME 04104-0658
U.S.A.

U.S Government Printing Office has a poster of the Everglades (stock number 024-005-00487-4). For information write to:
Superintendent of Documents
P.O. Box 371954
Pittsburgh, PA 15250-7954
U.S.A.

Wavelets is a set of 27 fact sheets with background information on marine topics. Wetlands sheets include salt marshes, brackish marshes, and freshwater wetlands. For information write to:
Sea Grant Communications
Virginia Institute of Marine Science
Gloucester Point, VA 23062
U.S.A.

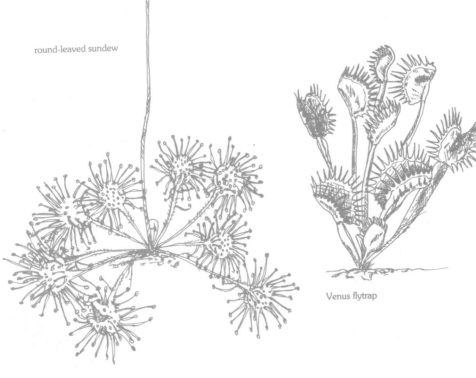

round-leaved sundew

Venus flytrap

OTHER ACTIVITY SOURCES

American Wetlands Month every May; offers brochures, posters, coloring books, buttons, stickers, and fact sheets with suggested activities, lists of educational materials, and wetland facts. For information write to:
American Wetlands Month
c/o Terrene Institute
1717 K St., N.W., Suite 801
Washington, DC 20006
U.S.A.

DEPTHS—Discovering Ecology: Pathways to Science (All grades) is a three-week curriculum focusing on estuarine ecology. Teacher workshops and teacher's manual available. For information write to:
Wells National Estuarine Research Reserve
342 Laudholm Farm Rd.
Wells, ME 04090-9988
U.S.A.

Marine Education: A Bibliography of Educational Materials Available from the Nation's Sea Grant Programs includes wetland-related publications and videos for all grade levels. For information write to:
Texas A&M University
Sea Grant Program
1716 Briarcrest, Suite 603
Bryan, TX 77802
U.S.A.

National Estuarine Research Reserve System (All grades) is a program of the 22 Reserves around the country that offer an extensive variety of curricula and other educational materials about estuaries. For the location of the Reserve nearest you, write:
Education and Outreach
Sanctuaries and Reserves Divs.
NOAA, 12th Floor
1305 East-West Hwy.
Silver Spring, MD 20910
U.S.A.

Wetlands Are Wonderlands (Advanced) are teacher and youth activity guides on freshwater wetlands. For information write to:
University of Illinois
Illinois-Indiana Sea Grant Publications
Attn. Cyndi Moore
67 Mumford Hall
1301 W. Gregory Dr.
Urbana, IL 61801
U.S.A.

A World in our Backyard: A Wetlands Education and Stewardship Program (Advanced) is a teaching package with two videos and a 140-page teacher's guide that introduces wetlands concepts and background information, describes experiments and activities, teaches wetland values, and offers school-community project ideas. For information write to:
Environmental Media
P.O. Box 1016
Chapel Hill, NC 27514
U.S.A.

or borrow from
EPA
Region 1 Library
JFK Federal Building
1 Congress St.
Boston, MA 02203-2211
U.S.A.

WOW: The Wonders of Wetlands (Primary to Advanced) is an educator's guide with 232 pages of background information and activities. For information east of the Mississippi write to:
Environmental Concern Inc.
P.O. Box P
St. Michaels, MD 21663-0480
U.S.A.

west of the Mississippi write to:
Project WET Fund-RDI
The Watercourse
Culbertson Hall
Montana State Univ.
Bozeman, MT 59717-0057
U.S.A.

Vernal Pools Lessons and Activities (Intermediate to Advanced) is a curriculum with hands-on activities about springtime wetlands and their conservation. For more information write to:
Massachusetts Audubon Society
Educational Resources
208 S. Great Rd.
Lincoln, MA 01773
U.S.A.

SOFTWARE

Earth's Endangered Environments is a CD-ROM, activity pages, and user's guide on wetlands and rain forests, including wetland life forms, importance, and effects of pollution and development. For a catalogue write to:
National Geographic Society
Educational Services
P.O. Box 98018
Washington, DC 20090-8018
U.S.A.

brine shrimp   89

WHERE TO GET MORE INFORMATION

- federal and state departments of parks, game and fish, natural resources, and wildlife
- local chapters of the Audubon Society, Ducks Unlimited, and the Izaak Walton League
- museums and nature centers
- state and local college and university departments of biology, ecology, and environmental science
- wildlife refuges
- World Wide Web site: U.S. Fish and Wildlife Service can be reached at http://www/fws.gov

Internet Address Disclaimer
The Internet information provided here was correct, to the best of our knowledge, at the time of publication. It is important to remember, however, the dynamic nature of the Internet. Resources that are free and publicly available one day may require a fee or restrict access the next, and the location of items may change as menus and homepages are reorganized.

fiddler crab